TIME

MANAGING EDITOR Nancy Gibbs
ART DIRECTOR D.W. Pine
DIRECTOR OF PHOTOGRAPHY Kira Pollack

Nelson Mandela: A Hero's Journey

EDITOR/WRITER Kelly Knauer
DESIGNER Ellen Fanning
PICTURE EDITOR Patricia Cadley
WRITER/RESEARCHER Matthew McCann Fenton
COPY EDITOR Bruce Christopher Carr

TIME HOME ENTERTAINMENT
PUBLISHER Jim Childs
VICE PRESIDENT, BRAND & DIGITAL STRATEGY Steven Sandonato
EXECUTIVE DIRECTOR, MARKETING SERVICES Carol Pittard
EXECUTIVE DIRECTOR, RETAIL & SPECIAL SALES Tom Mifsud
EXECUTIVE PUBLISHING DIRECTOR Joy Butts
DIRECTOR, BOOKAZINE DEVELOPMENT & MARKETING Laura Adam
FINANCE DIRECTOR Glenn Buonocore
PUBLISHING DIRECTOR Megan Pearlman
ASSOCIATE GENERAL COUNSEL Helen Wan
ASSISTANT DIRECTOR, SPECIAL SALES Ilene Schreider
BRAND MANAGER Bryan Christian
ASSOCIATE PRODUCTION MANAGER Kimberly Marshall
ASSOCIATE PREPRESS MANAGER Alex Voznesenskiy

EDITORIAL DIRECTOR Stephen Koepp
SENIOR EDITOR Roe D'Angelo
COPY CHIEF Rina Bander
DESIGN MANAGER Anne-Michelle Gallero
EDITORIAL OPERATIONS Gina Scauzillo

SPECIAL THANKS
Katherine Barnet, Brad Beatson, Jeremy Biloon, Dana Campolattaro, Susan Chodakiewicz, Rose Cirrincione, Natalie Ebel, Assu Etsubneh, Mariana Evans, Brian Fellows, Christine Font, Susan Hettleman, Hillary Hirsch, David Kahn, Amy Mangus, Nina Mistry, Dave Rozzelle, Ricardo Santiago, Adriana Tierno, Vanessa Wu, Time Inc. Premedia

ISBN 10: 1-61893-111-3
ISBN 13: 978-1-61893-111-5
Library of Congress Control Number: 2013942630

We welcome your comments and suggestions about Time Books. Please write to us at:
Time Books, Attention: Book Editors, P.O. Box 11016, Des Moines, IA 50336-1016.

If you would like to order any of our hardcover Collector's Edition books, please call us at:
800-327-6388, Monday through Friday, 7 a.m. to 8 p.m., or Saturday, 7 a.m. to 6 p.m., Central Time.

The people's choice *Mandela dons native garb on the campaign trail in his 1994 quest for the presidency*

Contents

Casting a long shadow *When South African blacks lined up in 1994 to vote in national elections for the first time, Nelson Mandela's vision of equality for all citizens began to be achieved*

The Reluctant Rebel

By Richard Stengel

■ ▬ ▬

N ELSON MANDELA WAS ALWAYS UNCOMFORTABLE TALKING ABOUT HIS own death. But not because he was afraid or in doubt. He was uncomfortable because he understood that people wanted him to offer homilies about death and he had none to offer. He was an utterly unsentimental man. I once asked him about his mortality while we were out walking one morning in the Transkei, the remote area of South Africa where he was born. He looked around at the green and tranquil landscape and said something about how he would be joining his "ancestors." "Men come and men go," he later said. "I have come and I will go when my time comes." And he seemed satisfied by that. I never once heard him mention God or heaven or any kind of afterlife. Nelson Mandela, who died at 95 on Dec. 5, 2013, in Johannesburg, believed in justice in this lifetime.

It was January of 1993 and I was working with him on his autobiography, *Long Walk to Freedom.* We had set out early that morning from the home near Qunu, the village of his father, that Mandela had built a few years after he was let out of prison. He had once said to me that every man should have a house in sight of where he was born. Much of Mandela's belief system came from his youth in the Xhosa tribe and being raised by a local Thembu King after his own father died. As a boy, he lived in a rondavel—a grass hut—with a dirt floor. He learned to be a shepherd. He fetched water from the spring. He excelled at stick fighting with the other boys. He sat at the feet of old men who told him stories of the brave African princes who ruled South Africa before the coming of the white man. The first time he ever shook the hand of a white man was when he went off to boarding school. Eventually, little Rolihlahla Mandela would become Nelson Mandela and get a proper Methodist education, but for all his worldliness and his legal training and the fine suits he liked to wear, much of his wisdom and common sense—and joy—came from what he had learned as a young boy in the Transkei.

Mandela might have been a more sentimental man if so much had not been taken away from him. His freedom. His ability to choose the path of his own life. His eldest son. The ability to live with his wife Winnie. Two great-grandchildren. Nothing in his life was permanent except the oppression he and his people were under. And everything he might have had he sacrificed to achieve the freedom of his people. But all the crude jailers, tiny cells and bumptious white apartheid leaders could not take away his pride, his dignity and his sense of justice. Even when he had to strip off his clothes and be hosed down when he first entered Robben Island, he stood

---

Richard Stengel is the former managing editor of TIME *magazine. He collaborated with Nelson Mandela in the writing of Mandela's acclaimed 1995 autobiography,* Long Walk to Freedom. *He is also the author of* Mandela's Way: Fifteen Lessons on Life, Love and Courage *(Crown; 2010).*

straight and did not complain. He refused to be intimidated in any circumstance. I remember interviewing Eddie Daniels, a 5-ft. 3-in. mixed-race freedom fighter who was in Cellblock B with Mandela on the island; Eddie recalled how anytime he felt demoralized, he would just have to see the 6-ft. 2-in. Mandela walking tall and straight through the courtyard and he would feel revived. Eddie wept as he told me how when he fell ill, Mandela—"Nelson Mandela, my leader!"—came into his cell and crouched down to wash out his pail of vomit and blood and excrement.

I always thought that in a different South Africa—a free and nonracial South Africa—Mandela would have been a small-town lawyer, content to be a local grandee. This great, historic revolutionary was in many ways a natural conservative. He liked ritual and tradition and did not believe in change for change's sake. But one thing turned him into a revolutionary, and that was the pernicious system of racial oppression he first experienced as a young man in Johannesburg. When people spat on him in buses, when shopkeepers turned him away, when whites treated him as if he could not read or write, that changed him irrevocably. For deep in his bones was a basic sense of fairness: he simply could not abide injustice. If he, Nelson Mandela, the son of a chief, tall, strong, handsome and educated, could be treated as subhuman, then what about the millions of his poor brothers and sisters who had nothing like his advantages? "That is not right," he would sometimes say to me about something as mundane as a plane flight's being canceled or as large as a world leader's policies, but that simple phrase—"That is not right"—underlay everything he did, everything he sacrificed for and everything he accomplished in his long and glorious life.

I saw him a handful of times over the past few years. He was much diminished. The extraordinary memory that could recall a particular dish at a dinner 60 years before was now such that he often did not recognize people he had known almost that long. But his pride and his regal bearing never left him. When he "retired from his retirement" (as he put it in 2004), I thought it was simply because he couldn't bear not remembering familiar things and he could not bear people seeing him in a way that did not live up to their expectations. He wanted people to see Nelson Mandela, and he was no longer the Nelson Mandela they wanted to see.

In many ways, the image of Nelson Mandela has become a kind of fairy tale: he is the last noble man, a figure of heroic scale and achievement. Indeed, his life has followed the narrative of the archetypal hero, of great suffering followed by redemption. But as he said to me and to many others over the years, "I am not a saint." And he wasn't. As a young revolutionary, he was not so gracious. He was fiery and rowdy and once tossed rival speakers off the podium. He originally wanted to exclude Indians and communists from the freedom struggle. He was the founder of Umkhonto we Sizwe (Spear of the Nation), the military wing of the African National Congress, and was considered the world's No. 1 terrorist in the early 1960s. He admired Gandhi, who started his own freedom struggle in South Africa in the 1890s, but as Mandela explained to me, he regarded nonviolence as a tactic, not a principle. If nonviolence was the most successful means to the end—the freedom of his people—he would embrace it. If it was not, he would abandon it. And he did. But like Gandhi, like Lincoln, like Churchill, he was doggedly, obstinately right about one overarching thing, and he never lost sight of that.

Prison was the crucible that formed the Mandela we know. The man who went into prison in 1962 was hotheaded and easily stung. The man who walked out into the sunshine of the mall in Cape Town 27 years later was measured, even serene. It was a hard-won moderation. In prison, he learned to control his emotions and his anger. He had no choice. He learned patience, be-

This great, historic revolutionary was in many ways a natural conservative. He liked ritual and tradition and did not believe in change for change's sake. But one thing turned him into a revolutionary, and that was the pernicious system of racial oppression he first experienced as a young man in Johannesburg.

cause he had to. And he came to understand that if he was ever to achieve the free and nonracial South Africa of his dreams, he would have to come to terms with his oppressors. He would have to forgive them. After I asked him many times during our weeks and months of conversation what was different about the man who came out of prison compared with the man who went in, he finally sighed and then said simply, "I came out mature."

His greatest achievement is surely the creation of a modern, democratic, nonracial South Africa and preventing that beautiful country from falling into a terrible, bloody civil war. Several years after I finished working with him on *Long Walk to Freedom,* he told me that he wanted to write another book, about how close South Africa had been to a race war. I was with him in 1993 at the moment he got the news that black South African leader Chris Hani had been assassinated, probably the closest the country came to going to war. He was preternaturally calm, and after making plans to go to Johannesburg to speak to the nation, he methodically finished eating his breakfast of porridge and fruit. To prevent that civil war, he had to use all the skills in his head and his heart: he had to demonstrate rocklike strength to the Afrikaner leaders with whom he was negotiating but also show that he was not out for revenge. And he had to show his people that he was not compromising with the enemy. This was an incredibly delicate line to walk—and from the outside, he seemed to do it with grace. But it took its toll.

And because he was not a saint, he had his share of bitterness. He famously said, "The struggle is my life," but his life was also a struggle. This man who loved children spent 27 years without holding a baby. In the years before he went to prison, he was hunted and lived underground and was unable to be the father and the husband he wanted to be. I remember his telling me that when he was known as the Black Pimpernel and was being pursued by thousands of policemen, he secretly went to see his son to tuck him into bed. His son asked him why he couldn't be with him every night, and Mandela told him that millions of other South African children needed him too. So many people have said to me over the years, "It's amazing that he was not bitter." I've always smiled at that. With enormous self-control, he learned to hide his bitterness.

And then, after he had forged this new South Africa, won the first democratic election in the country's history, formed a government and began to redress the historical wrongs done to his people, he walked away from it. He became the rarest thing in African history, a one-term President who chose not to run for office again. Like George Washington, he understood that every step he made would be a template for others to follow. He could have been President for life, but he knew that for democracy to rule, he could not. Two democratic elections have followed his presidency, and if the men who have succeeded him have not been his equal, well, that too is democracy. He was a large man in every way. His legacy is that he expanded human freedom. He was tolerant of everything but intolerance. He deserves to rest in peace.

A Life in Pictures
Nelson Mandela

What's in a name? *Rolihlahla Mandela was given the name Nelson Mandela, most likely in honor of Britain's legendary admiral, Horatio Nelson, when he attended a British-oriented Methodist school as a boy*

Youngster

The trajectory of Nelson Mandela's life closely parallels that of the nation of South Africa: it is the story of a journey from the country to the city, from ancient ways to modern ways, from a colonial society strictly segregated by race to a free, multiracial nation.

Rolihlalah Mandela was born on July 18, 1918, in a circular thatched hut in a village, or kraal, in the agricultural Transkei region of South Africa's Eastern Cape province. Mandela's clan, the Thembu, were of noble blood in his tribe, the Xhosa; his father Gadla Henry Mphakanyiswa was a counselor to the Xhosa king, David Jongintaba Dalindyebo, who became the boy's guardian after his father died when he was 9.

A bright student, Mandela entered a mission school at age 7, where he was given the name Nelson. He excelled in Western-style schools, but at age 19 he was asked to leave Fort Hare University in Alice in the Eastern Cape province, for leading protests against school policies.

Defying Jongintaba, who had arranged a marriage for Mandela to a Xhosa bride he didn't love, the young man fled to Johannesburg, where he worked briefly in a mine, then became a clerk in a law office while taking classes to complete his university and law degrees.

There are no photographs of Mandela before his late teens. The picture at right was taken in 1978, but it shows rituals of a boy's life in the Transkei that appear to be little changed from those of Mandela's boyhood 50 years before.

Lawyer and Activist

Had he been born in a different nation, Nelson Mandela might have become a wealthy Establishment lawyer. But racial injustice in South Africa—where a small minority of white British and Dutch residents (Afrikaners) ruled a vast majority of uneducated and impoverished native blacks with a very firm hand—drove him to become an activist for black rights.

In 1944, influenced by the nonviolent methods of India's Mohandas Gandhi, Mandela, his college friend Oliver Tambo and others founded the Youth League of the African National Congress (A.N.C.), one of the nation's oldest black rights groups. Four years later the Afrikaner-dominated Parliament passed laws instituting the system of apartheid, the strict separation of South Africa by race. The laws marginalized black South Africans in their own land, and Mandela devoted himself to their overthrow. Tall, imposing, brilliant, a Xhosa nobleman and a natty dresser, he became one of apartheid's most effective foes.

By the mid-1950s the A.N.C. was leading effective protests and boycotts against the hated policy. The government clamped down: Mandela and 155 others were charged with treason in 1956. The show trial dragged on for five years; in the end, no defendants were found guilty. Left, Mandela joins supporters in a protest song during the Treason Trial.

BARRY VON BELOW

9

DAILY TELEGRAPH—UK

Prisoner

By the early 1960s South Africans lived in a state of permanent crisis, as a new wave of black consciousness and pride swept across all of Africa. Mandela's African National Congress, pledged to nonviolence and a multiracial future for the nation, was challenged by more militant black organizations, while the South African government turned the nation into an increasingly brutal police state in order to enforce minority white rule. Matters came to a climax in the Sharpeville Massacre in March 1960, when white police killed 69 unarmed black protesters and injured more than 180. After angry blacks rioted across the land, the government outlawed the A.N.C., driving its leaders underground.

Convinced their nonviolent strategy was failing, Mandela and a few A.N.C. allies formed a militant wing of the group, Umkhonto we Sizwe (Spear of the Nation), and began plotting a sabotage campaign against the state. Now living on the run as a wanted rebel, Mandela toured Africa to learn guerrilla-warfare skills, while newspapers dubbed him the Black Pimpernel. But he was arrested on Aug. 5, 1962 and put on trial with other A.N.C. leaders; ultimately he was given a life sentence. In June 1964 he began serving his term in the Robben Island prison outside Cape Town; at left he speaks in the prison yard in 1965 with his longtime A.N.C. colleague Walter Sisulu. For this photo-op for the British press—the first and last of its kind—the prisoners were issued adequate clothing for a few hours.

1964	1973	1982
1965	1974	1983
1966	1975	1984
1967	1976	1985
1968	1977	1986
1969	1978	1987
1970	1979	1988
1971	1980	1989
1972	1981	**1990**

The Dark Years

Sentenced to life in prison at age 44,
Nelson Mandela was not set free until
he was 71. Only a very few photos were
taken of him during those long years,
and by state law, it was illegal to publish them. What you see on these pages
is what South Africans saw of Nelson
Mandela between 1964 and 1990. Yet if
the political prisoner's face was never
seen, his presence was inescapable:
hidden from sight, Mandela became
a symbol, a larger-than-life figure, a
phantom who came to embody the struggle against apartheid.

Over the course of 27 years, this single
powerless prisoner came to seem more
powerful than all the state's men and
guns. His cause attracted followers
around the globe, as a swelling chorus
of voices called for his release and for the
abolition of apartheid. Nations backed
up those entreaties with tough economic
sanctions, corporations by withdrawing their investments. At home, his
followers made good on their threat to
make their nation ungovernable until he
was released. Finally, on Feb. 11, 1990,
South Africa's leaders conceded their
error: they heeded the rallying cry of
millions around the globe—Free Nelson
Mandela!—and the world saw the famed
prisoner's face, for the first time in more
than a quarter-century.

ALLAN TANNENBAUM—CORBIS SYGMA

Free at Last!

On Feb. 11, 1990, the world held its breath as Nelson Mandela walked out of South Africa's Victor Verster Prison—finally free after his long years in jail as a political prisoner. During that time, Mandela had become the foremost symbol of the struggle against the racist system of apartheid, a struggle that was embraced not only by his fellow blacks in South Africa but also by a swelling tide of individuals, businesses and governments around the world.

His party, the African National Congress, skillfully manipulated Mandela's imprisonment to rally world opinion in favor of his release, even as it waged a successful campaign to make South Africa ungovernable until that day arrived. In the last years before he was freed, the nation often seemed on the verge of a violent showdown in which blacks and whites would fight to the death in a bloodbath.

In the end, it was the prisoner, not his jailers, who held the reins of power. Mandela was set free because he was the only figure who could conceivably lead South Africa to a peaceful future, in which apartheid would be abolished and all citizens would be recognized as equals. At his side in his moment of triumph was his wife Winnie, who had been a pillar of support during his long ordeal. Sadly, their marriage would fail in the bright light of freedom.

LOUISE GUBB—THE IMAGE WORKS

Leader

Released from jail after serving more than 25 years as a political prisoner, Nelson Mandela faced an Everest of expectations. While in prison, he had become more symbol than man; he now carried the hopes of most South Africans on his back. Somehow, it was believed, Mandela would find a way to unite his deeply divided nation, walking it back from decades of anger, turmoil and bloodshed and re-creating it as a multiracial society with equal rights for all.

Improbably, that's exactly what he did. Immediately after his release, he declared he would never abandon his commitment to equal rights for all citizens. He also explained that he would pursue a policy of reconciliation: he would seek justice, not revenge, for the brutalities visited by whites against blacks under apartheid.

Mandela's firm claim to moral greatness rests upon this expansive, liberating vision. But to apply it, he had to work through the political system. And he did, negotiating with a master's touch with the man who freed him, President F.W. de Klerk, to manage the nation's gradual evolution to equal citizenship for all.

In 1994, in the first national election in which black South Africans were able to vote, Mandela thrilled the world by campaigning, left, under the once outlawed banner of the African National Congress and winning election as the nation's first black President.

Ambassador

Nelson Mandela, who was freed from prison at age 71 and became South Africa's first black President at age 75, served only a single term, taking office on May 10, 1994, and yielding it to his chosen successor, Thabo Mbeki, in 1999.

The onetime political prisoner had become one of the world's most honored and beloved citizens. Mandela had been so out of touch with the changing times during his long imprisonment that when he first emerged from prison he recoiled from fuzzy microphones extended on long booms by camera crews, fearing they were weapons. Now, both as South Africa's President and in the years after his retirement, he became an up-to-date citizen of the world, whose famous smile beamed from millions of T shirts, coffee mugs, refrigerator magnets and, eventually, YouTube videos.

At right, Mandela meets with the Dalai Lama in 1996. Following his retirement, he joined the Elders, a group of veteran public servants, including Archbishop Desmond Tutu and former U.S. President Jimmy Carter, who sought to provide counsel on a variety of issues of global concern.

SASA KRALJ—AP/WIDE WORLD

Elder Statesman

In 2004—five years after he stepped down as President of South Africa and seven years after the photograph at right captured him revisiting his boyhood haunts in the Transkei—Nelson Mandela announced he would withdraw from public life to focus his political efforts on a single cause: the fight against HIV/AIDS, which had reached epidemic proportions in South Africa and would claim the life of his son Makgatho in 2005.

The former prisoner was now able to devote himself to pleasures long denied. The father of five, whose political career had denied him time to spend with his own children, now doted on his grandchildren. On his 80th birthday, the man whose two marriages had failed, also victims of politics, wed Graça Machel, widow of President Samora Machel of Mozambique.

His great work was done: during his long ordeal in prison, he had become apartheid's scapegoat, taking the sins, fears and burdens of an entire nation on his back—and he had expiated them upon his release through his determined embrace of reconciliation and his remarkable freedom from rancor. The father of modern South Africa deserved to have his name spoken along with those of history's great liberators: Lincoln and Gandhi and King. But his countrymen preferred to call him by a special name: "Madiba," a Thembu term awarded only to the most beloved of elders.

LOUISE GUBB—CORBIS SABA

One Land, Many Peoples

BARTOLOMEU DIAS, THE PIONEERING Portuguese navigator who was the first European explorer to round the southern tip of Africa, named the forbidding, wind-whipped passage between the Atlantic and Indian oceans *El Cabo de Todos los Tormentos*—the Cape of All Storms. And for centuries to follow, seamen battling the famously howling winds and turbulent seas of the transcontinental passage—considered the single most dangerous transit for seafarers on the planet—would agree with Dias. But someone more important didn't agree: when Dias returned to Lisbon, his patron, King John II, overruled him. In an inspired burst of early Renaissance spin doctoring, he rechristened the tail end of Africa *El Cabo da Boa Esperança:* the Cape of Good Hope.

King John's more sanguine name sprang from his delight at having found a sea route to India, which promised domination of the burgeoning spice trade and with it, untold riches. But the belief that southern Africa was no more than a way station to the wealth of the Orient would shape the region's history for centuries. When Vasco da Gama followed Dias' path in 1498 and eventually navigated all the way to India, he didn't bother to stop in the forbidding, rocky land we now call South Africa on either leg of his journey.

Gold! *Above, bosses and workers gather at a gold mine in*

BETTMANN CORBIS

De Kaap, circa 1888. The discovery of diamonds and gold accelerated European immigration and placed many native South Africans in servitude

Had he bothered to stop and explore Africa's southern tip, Da Gama would have found a thriving mix of diverse tribal cultures whose members often traded, sometimes made war and always engaged in a lively exchange of ideas and technology. Indeed, recently uncovered archaeological evidence suggests that proto-human hominids first migrated to the area around 3 million years ago. About 1 million years ago, they were displaced by *Homo erectus,* a hominid species that was in turn supplanted by *Homo sapiens* around 100,000 years ago. These first modern humans in southern Africa eventually formed the early Bushman and Bantu cultures. In the latter language group, the word *Bantu* simply means "people," implying that these tribesmen were as blithely unaware of the civilization outside their ken as Dias, Da Gama and the other Europeans who followed were uninterested in theirs.

For more than 150 years, no European power would attempt to establish a colony in southern Africa, until a Dutch vessel foundered in the harbor now called Table Bay in 1647. The survivors came ashore, built a fort and remained at the site of modern-day Cape Town for a year before being rescued. Within four years, the Dutch East India Company, the giant firm that replaced the Portuguese as the primary explorers and traders on the Spice Route, decided that the hazardous Cape of Good Hope required a permanent settlement at which ships plying the seas to India and Asia could put in for repairs and provisions.

From their first arrival in southern Africa, the Dutch set a pattern in dealing with the natives that would endure for centuries: they demanded food, fresh water and timber for ship repairs, then reacted violently when the local Khoisan peoples (a branch of the Bushman people) refused. With their superior weapons, the Dutch drove the Khoisans many miles away from the coast. The land thus vacated was quickly settled by Dutch farmers, who were assisted by African slaves brought in by ship from elsewhere on the continent. In the years that followed, Dutch and German farmers and ranchers, who called themselves Afrikaners, would flock to the new colony, followed in 1688 by thousands of French Huguenots fleeing the anti-Protestant persecution of King Louis XIV. The rich land they settled soon yielded great wealth, chiefly in the form of wine and wheat. The blacks they displaced were incorporated into the growing white economy as servants or unskilled, inexpensive labor.

The result was a combustible mix of European settlers who felt little kinship for one another, surrounded by resentful native Africans who were either enslaved, driven from their land—or both—by white foreigners. Further tension was created by the monopolistic trading practices of the Dutch East India Company, which left many Afrikaner farmers, or Boers, feeling cheated by what they saw as unfair prices. They moved further inland, outside the company's jurisdiction, displacing more natives in the process. Thus were born the Trekboers, or Wandering Farmers. In time they would establish several short-lived republics that declared their independence from European colonial control.

ENTER BRITAIN

During the next century, the sun set on the Netherlands' pre-eminence in the spice trade and dominance as a colonial power, much as it had on Portugal's before. The British stepped in, seizing the Dutch settlements in southern Africa in 1795 to prevent them from falling into the hands of Britain's new principal rival, the French. For 20 years, London attempted to appease the largely Dutch population of the region, recruiting disgruntled Dutch settlers as allies. In 1814, however, Britain formally annexed southern Africa as the Cape Colony. Along

Migration *The Voortrek, or Great Trek, began in 1835, as Boers fled British rule to pioneer new homesteads in South Africa's interior regions. The picture above shows Boer farmers on the move later in the 19th century*

with their new turf, the British inherited an old problem: Dutch settlers, already resentful of control by their own countrymen, were even less likely to accept rule by British masters. Aiming to dilute Dutch influence, the Crown encouraged thousands of British farmers and businessmen to immigrate to South Africa. Many of them were settled in a rural war zone, intended to act as buffers between the Dutch farmers and the Xhosa tribesmen they were attempting to displace. This unrealistic plan was an utter failure. The British settlers soon retreated to the large cities, and a new source of instability and resentment was layered on top of South Africa's tinderbox social structure: henceforth, Dutch-speaking farmers would fear and loathe English-speaking city dwellers, who soon came to dominate the colony's commerce, culture and government.

THE VOORTREK

A precarious situation tilted further toward disaster when the British decided in 1833 to abolish slavery in the Cape Colony. The Boers viewed this as tantamount to a declaration of war, for their livelihoods depended on agriculture sustained by the free labor of slaves. From this vortex sprang the Voortrek, or Great Trek. A larger version of the earlier Trekboer movement, this mass migration by Boers to the inland countryside was conducted this time to evade

British, rather than Dutch, control. Whereas the earlier movement had displaced individual clans, this tidal wave of settlers threatened to uproot entire nations of indigenous Africans.

Conflict and carnage were the inevitable result. In 1838 the Voortrekkers used their superior arms to massacre so many Zulu tribesmen that the Ncome River is reported to have briefly run red. Ever since, it has been known as the Blood River. Moving north and east, the migrating Boers established several small new nations: the Natalia Republic, the Transvaal Republic and the Orange Free State. Hoping to stem this tide, the British passed the Masters and Servants law in 1841, which formalized white control and strictly limited black rights: it was slavery in a new suit of clothes. By the late 1840s, an uneasy peace held sway in southern Africa: Cape Colonists didn't recognize the independence of the new Boer nations but left them alone, for they were not threatened by small, minor republics located on worthless land outside their borders.

GOLD RUSH

Then, in 1866, everything changed. A shiny white pebble was found in the Vaal River, on the border between the Transvaal Republic and the Orange Free State. It was a 21-carat diamond. Within a few years, the areas occupied by Boers would emerge as the largest, richest source of diamonds in the world; they remain so today. A few years later, staggeringly rich deposits of gold were found in the same area. Tens of thousands—then hundreds of thousands—of blacks were brought into the gold and diamond mines to provide cheap labor.

The British, ears attuned to the reveille of riches, quickly reconsidered their indifference to Boer independence. Moving swiftly to annex the newly valuable territory to the north and east of the Cape Colony, the British attempted to subjugate the Boer nations and begin the process of exploiting their mineral wealth. In the brutal Boer Wars that followed, the British won control of the Boer republics, as recognized in the 1902 Treaty of Vereeniging.

The Boers' resentment of their plight, never quite extinguished, was rekindled when the British quickly began trying to Anglicize and unify the population by making English the official language in the Cape Colony. Colonial overseers also moved to depress wages, especially among miners, by importing tens of thousands of Indian and Chinese laborers into a country already torn by racial division. Making matters worse, the British imposed new taxes designed both to discourage black natives from voting and encourage them to leave farms and take jobs in the mines. That led, in 1906, to the Bambatha Rebellion, named for the Zulu chief who exhorted his followers to resist both injunctions. The uprising culminated in a battle in which British troops slaughtered more than 4,000 Zulus.

These troubles with native blacks led the British to embrace their fellow whites, the Boers. In 1910 the Act of Union consolidated all territory in South Africa to form a new independent nation of the British Empire, the Union of South Africa. In an attempt to stave off civil war, Boers were given a limited measure of "home rule," while both Dutch and English were named official languages. Most important to the ardently white-supremacist Boers, voting and the eligibility to hold public office remained limited to whites only—in spite of the fact that black or partially black residents by then made up more than 75% of the British colony's population. Widespread outrage at this injustice gave rise to the first meaningful black opposition that crossed old ethnic and tribal boundaries. In the years that followed in this unnatural racial maelstrom—as black resolution stiffened and white inflexibility hardened—the land that Bartolomeu Dias had called the Cape of All Storms began to live up to its name.

Three Different Worlds

Native Africans

When Europeans first arrived in what is now South Africa, they encountered two principal groups of black natives: the Bushmen, a collection of hunter-gatherer tribes, and the Bantu, an advanced, agrarian civilization of farmers and ranchers. The Bantu group included several large nations, including the Zulu (left), the Basotho and the Xhosa, Nelson Mandela's tribe. The Zulu, a people comprised of more than 400 tribes and dozens of separate but related languages, are the largest ethnic group in South Africa; they have frequently been rivals of the Xhosa, with the smaller Xhosa tribe suffering displacement from Zulu expansion in the 19th century. This contentious relationship continued into the 20th century, when the Zulu nation opposed Mandela's leadership and formed a rival black resistance group, the Inkatha Freedom Party.

The Afrikaners

A quick glossary: all descendants of South Africa's original Dutch colonizers are known as Afrikaners; farming Afrikaners, particularly those who moved inland in the Great Trek, are Boers; Afrikaners who stayed near the original coastal settlements of South Africa call themselves Cape Dutch. Afrikaners tend to be Protestant (especially Calvinist); over four centuries, their language evolved into its own, distinct dialect of Dutch, Afrikaans. While their mother country came to be regarded as a haven of diversity and openness, Afrikaners evolved their own political and social outlook that emphasized a defiant pride in their language and culture (they bitterly resisted British attempts to make English the national language of South Africa) and a firm belief that white racial superiority was divinely ordained. At various times, large groups of Afrikaners have left South Africa, usually in response to political setbacks, and immigrated en masse to found new communities in lands as close as Kenya and as far away as Argentina and Mexico.

The British

Britons, late-comers to South Africa, never quite seemed to understand the complex political and social dynamics of the powder keg over which they presided. Whether trying to impose the English language on Dutch settlers or demanding that proud Zulu kings pay fealty to the British Crown, these ambivalent overlords were perpetually mystified by their subjects. They even believed that the colony's simmering racial tensions would somehow be eased when they imported thousands of laborers from elsewhere in the British Empire (especially India, Malaysia and China)—and then treated them as second-class citizens, one notch above the native blacks. The British remained outsiders, a tiny minority presiding unsteadily over a society defined and divided by one criterion: race.

The price of empire *British soldiers rest and recuperate after a battle with Boers in Driefontein, near Johannesburg*

The Wars of the Boers

The discovery of gold and diamonds lured British miners and prospectors by the tens of thousands to southern Africa in the 1870s. But the riches they sought were located in lands controlled by the descendants of Dutch settlers, the Boers of the Transvaal Republic and the Orange Free State, who denied the *uitlanders* (foreigners) within their borders the right to vote and taxed them heavily. These policies ratcheted up tensions, and in January 1877, with the Transvaal Republic approaching anarchy, Britain formally annexed the state.

The First Boer War began in December 1880, when Boers in turn declared independence for the Transvaal. British troops engaged Boer guerrilla fighters for the next 14 months, but in a replay of the American Revolution, the imperial troops were no match for local Afrikaners fighting for their land, and they suffered several humiliating routs. The British, humbled, finally agreed to self-government for the Transvaal, buying both sides a few years of peace.

Tensions flared again in 1895 when the archetypal British imperialist, Cecil Rhodes, founder of the De Beers diamond cartel, financed an attempted coup in the Transvaal. Although the putsch failed to topple the government, it awakened the interest of Germany, then an expanding colonial power, which began shipping arms to Boer militants, the Germans' ethnic compatriots.

The Second Boer War broke out in December 1899, with the British bent on displaying whatever ruthlessness victory required. They adopted a scorched-earth policy, torching Boer villages and farms, exiling more than 20,000 prisoners of war to points as far away as Bermuda and India and herding Boer women and children into concentration camps, where they died by the tens of thousands of starvation, disease and exposure.

In May 1902, the thoroughly beaten Boers relented and sued for peace. Eight years later the Transvaal Republic and Orange Free State were absorbed into the British Empire. Control of South Africa and its mineral wealth was now finally and completely in the hands of the British.

NELSON MANDELA'S SOUTH AFRICA

Capitals: Pretoria ....administrative
Cape Town ....legislative
Bloemfontein ....judicial

Area: 470,693 sq. mi. (1,219,090 sq. km.)
Population (2007): 47,851,000
Ethnic composition: black 78%; white 10%; mixed race 9%; Asian 3%

300 mi.

Source: TIME Almanac

ZIMBABWE

MOZAMBIQUE

Limpopo River

LIMPOPO

• Pietersburg

BOTSWANA

Gaborone ⌖

Liliesleaf Farm, ANC hideout

MPUMALANGA

Pretoria ⌖
GAUTENG   Nelspruit •

Maputo ⌖

• Mafeking

Krugersdorp•   Johannesburg

NORTH WEST   Soweto•   •Brakpan

Evaton•

Klerksdorp •   •Vereeniging

SWAZILAND

NAMIBIA

• Upington

Kimberley •

Welkom •

Virginia •

KWAZULU/NATAL

FREE STATE

⌖
Bloemfontein

LESOTHO

Mandela arrested, 8/5/62

Pietermaritzburg•   •Durban
                        Amanzimtoti

NORTHERN CAPE

Orange River

South Atlantic Ocean

S O U T H   A F R I C A

Drakensberg Range

•Port Shepstone
Port Edward •

Indian Ocean

EASTERN CAPE   Qunu •   Mandela birthplace

Alice •   Fort Hare, Mandela's University

Robben Island prison

WESTERN CAPE

East London

Paarl •

Cape Town ⌖   Victor Verster Prison

Uitenhage•
                 • Port Elizabeth

Cape of Good Hope

Pollsmoor Prison

South Africa : A Timeline

1487
Portuguese navigator Bartolomeu Dias circumnavigates the Cape of Good Hope

1652
The Dutch erect a fort at today's Cape Town. During the next 140 years, they will engage in a number of Wars of Dispossession with native tribes to widen their area of control, while smallpox decimates indigenous populations

1795
As Dutch fortunes wane, Britain assumes control of the Dutch colony at Cape Town

1814
Britain formally annexes the Dutch colony and names it Cape Colony

1833
The Voortrek begins: Dutch settlers migrate north and east after Britain outlaws slavery, founding new republics

1866
Gold is discovered in the Transvaal

1880-81; 1899-1902
In the Boer Wars, Britain defeats the Dutch republics surrounding the Cape Colony

1910
Cape Colony gives way to the Union of South Africa, a dominion of the British empire

1924
The African National Congress is founded to advance native rights

1949-1950s
Ruling National Party legislates "grand apartheid," enforcing segregation and forcing blacks to live in Bantustan "homelands"

1956-1961
Mandela and 155 other defendants are tried and acquitted in the Treason Trial; 1960's Sharpeville Massacre divides nation

1962-64
Mandela, now a militant guerrilla, is captured and sentenced to life in prison in 1964

1976
Soweto Uprising inflames racial divisions; activist Stephen Biko is murdered in 1977

1980s
Antiapartheid forces grow in power as other nations place sanctions on South Africa, while the nation erupts in further racial violence

1990
Mandela released from prison

1994
Nelson Mandela elected president in first vote to include South Africans of all races. He serves a single five-year term

MAP BY JOE LERTOLA

Apartheid:
A Tale of Two Nations

◼▬▬▬

ARLY IN THE 20TH CENTURY, BRITAIN WAS THE WORLD'S GREATEST power, presiding over a vast colonial realm on which the sun, famously, never set. But as the century progressed, the tides of history flowed against the pillars of empire: colonialism, racism and European hegemony. Around the world, subject peoples declared their independence from colonial powers and fought to secure their sovereignty, while oppressed racial minorities everywhere battled for equality and justice. Yet one nation, South Africa, defied history's momentum for decades, as the descendants of white European immigrants erected stronger and stronger barriers against the native blacks, even at the cost of transforming their land into a brutal police state that was reviled and shunned by other nations. Defiant in their adherence to racism, South Africa's white leaders eventually enshrined their prejudices in the nation's lawbooks under the system they called apartheid, a Dutch term meaning "separateness."

As the 20th century dawned, South Africa's British rulers seem to have believed that the experiment in nation building they succeeded in putting into place in 1910—the new Union of South Africa—would finally put the lid on the bubbling cauldron of racial tensions they had presided over for 115 years. The British could not have been more mistaken.

A generation of South Africa's black leaders had grown up with at least the right to vote and the opportunity to be educated. But in a concession by the British to placate Afrikaners, the new nation's laws and policies effectively deprived blacks of both. For their part, Dutch-speaking South Africans continued to resent British rule, for although the union was technically an independent nation, it also remained a dominion of the United Kingdom. The Afrikaners were also deeply suspicious of blacks' growing interest in improving their circumstances. The

Compare and contrast *Top, a member of a whites-only club in 1990; below, a street scene in the township of New Brighton, 1985*

Dutch speakers blamed the British: since the 1890s, these bearers of the "white man's burden" had allowed talented black youth not only to be educated by European missionaries, but even to journey abroad for studies at élite universities. In fearing educated blacks, the Afrikaners could not have been more correct.

In January 1912, one such student, Pixley ka Isaka Seme, a Zulu prince who had attended universities in the U.S. and Britain, allied himself with John Langalibalele Dube, a native black missionary who had graduated from Oberlin College in Ohio, where he had been deeply influenced by the teachings of Booker T. Washington. After returning to the U.S., the two men teamed up with Solomon Tshekisho Plaatje, a black intellectual and writer who had also traveled to the U.S., to found the South African Native National Congress, with Dube as its first president. Its goal: improved conditions for all South Africa's blacks.

The nascent movement gathered steam during World War I, when a soaring demand for labor led to the temporary relaxation of the rules against black workers' holding jobs reserved for whites. As a result, vast townships, essentially black-only ghettos, sprang up around white cities where jobs were plentiful, such as Johannesburg. Yet as soon as the war ended, white legislators rolled back black avenues to advancement, passing numerous restrictive racial laws that made it illegal for black workers to strike, reserved skilled jobs for whites, barred blacks from military service and instituted internal travel restrictions for black citizens.

Within a decade, the organization Seme, Dube and Plaatje had founded had a new name, the African National Congress, or A.N.C., and a new sense of urgency. In 1924, the most racist of Afrikaner parties, the National Party, came to power as part of a coalition government. While British rule had been onerous for black South Africans, it had always been restrained in comparison to the kind of discrimination hoped for by the new regime: racial bigotry codified and required under law, rather than merely permitted by social custom.

THE BLACK THREAT

The centerpiece of the National Party agenda was dealing with the *swart gevaar*—Dutch for "black threat." The party quickly instituted a program called "civilized labor," which banned black unions while recognizing those with white membership; increased the number of white voters (chiefly by granting the franchise to women) while placing further legal restrictions on black voting; and empowered the government to force private employers to give preference to white applicants over blacks. The government-sanctioned repression was brutal, yet for decades after it was founded, the A.N.C. and its well-educated leaders answered South Africa's increasingly harsh policies of segregation with petitions, orderly public meetings and appeals for justice phrased so politely that they could easily have been mistaken for requests.

While black leaders dithered, a population time bomb was ticking. Although English-speaking South Africans dominated the government and business sectors, they were a numerically smaller group than the descendants of Dutch settlers. The influence of the more tolerant British, strong in the early years of the union, waned steadily over the decades. The watershed election of 1948 handed outright control of Parliament to the National Party, which had advocated supporting Nazi Germany during World War II. In the campaign, its candidates ran on such slogans as *Die Kaffir op Sy Plek* ("The Nigger in His Place") and "*Die Koelies Uit die Land* ("The Coolies Out of the Country")—a reference to immigrant Indians, who formed another large and disenfranchised ethnic block within South Africa.

The Many Villages of Apartheid

Although Bantu translates simply as "human being" in hundreds of languages spoken by tribes native to South Africa, Afrikaners employed the word as a derogatory term for blacks. Linked with the Persian suffix -*stan* ("country"), it became the name for one of apartheid's most squalid creations—the regions carved out of scrubland by the white regime, into which almost all South Africa's blacks were herded.

Such "black homelands"(an Afrikaner euphemism for the Bantustans) had existed unofficially since the 1930s, but the first of them was formally sanctioned in 1962. Even before that, whites began driving blacks away from white cities, beginning with the forced removal of some 65,000 blacks from Sophiatown, near Johannesburg, in 1955, as seen at left below. The A.N.C. fought the removals, without success. By the mid-1970s, nine other reserves were set aside within South Africa, along with 10 more in the territory of South West Africa (now the nation of Namibia but then under the control of South Africa). These arid, erosion-riddled wastelands were incapable of supporting large populations. No matter: some 80% of the country's residents were eventually forced into them. At right below are black students and a teacher in a Bantu school.

In the 1970s these ersatz nations were granted their "independence" by South Africa. This legal fiction, recognized by no other nation in the world, formally stripped most of South Africa's blacks of citizenship in their native land. The Bantustans survived until 1994, when both apartheid and its bogus homelands were dissolved.

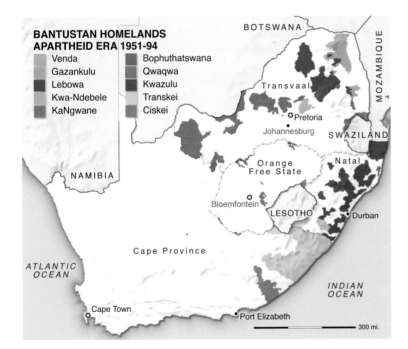

BANTUSTAN HOMELANDS APARTHEID ERA 1951-94

- Venda
- Gazankulu
- Lebowa
- Kwa-Ndebele
- KaNgwane
- Bophuthatswana
- Qwaqwa
- Kwazulu
- Transkei
- Ciskei

BOTSWANA

MOZAMBIQUE

Transvaal

⊕ Pretoria
• Johannesburg
SWAZILAND

NAMIBIA

Orange Free State
Natal

✪ Bloemfontein
LESOTHO
• Durban

Cape Province

ATLANTIC OCEAN

INDIAN OCEAN

✪ Cape Town
• Port Elizabeth

300 mi.

LEFT: BOB GOSANI—DRUM SOCIAL HISTORIES—BAILEY'S AFRICAN HISTORY ARCHIVE—AFRICANPICTURES.NET; RIGHT: PETER MAGUBANE—DRUM SOCIAL HISTORIES—BAILEY'S AFRICAN HISTORY ARCHIVE—AFRICANPICTURES.NET; MAP BY JOE LERTOLA

LAW AND BORDERS

No longer tempered by the restraining influence of having to govern as part of a coalition, South Africa's new National Party administration quickly began creating a systematic policy of apartheid that expanded the nation's traditional social segregation, giving it statutory form and force. Hendrik F. Verwoerd, who became Minister of Native Affairs in 1950, is often credited with being the architect of apartheid—a designation that is only partially correct, although Verwoerd might have been flattered by it.

Every person in the country was soon required to be officially classified by race, with non-whites compelled to carry identity papers, or passbooks, at all times. Apartheid's broad, official embrace of discrimination set up an elaborate system of racial tiers: those not white were carefully categorized as blacks, Indians or mixed-race coloureds. Under this pecking order of racial fanaticism, the last two groups, whose blood Afrikaners viewed as less tainted, enjoyed more privileges than those deemed least worthy, native blacks. The result was a social pyramid in which a minority of whites, who represented some 20% of the nation's population, occupied 85% of the nation's land and ruled firmly over the remaining 80% of the population. Nonwhite South Africans were now ensured a future of unequal justice under law.

The nation's new leaders turned out to be more ruthlessly determined to repress black Africans than even the most militant A.N.C. activists had feared. Under the Group Areas Act of 1950, apartheid's embrace extended to geography. Parliament officially created all-white enclaves in which all other races were prohibited to live, work or even visit without government permission. Native blacks, whom Afrikaners called Bantus, were herded into utterly artificial "homelands," or Bantustans, and forced to produce their passbooks in order to travel into white-occupied territories.

Apartheid's zealots also cracked down on black education, for by the late 1950s, it was clear that nearly every black leader who resisted apartheid was the product of advanced schooling. The National Party pushed through legislation that closed black schools, prohibited white schools from admitting blacks and discouraged religious organizations and their missionary teachers from educating blacks. Verwoerd, who became Prime Minister in 1961, argued, "What is the use of teaching a Bantu child mathematics when it cannot use it in practice? Education must train and teach people in accordance with their opportunities in life." In a moment of stark candor, he also said, "There is no place for [the Bantu] in the European community above certain forms of labor."

A HOUSE DIVIDED

Nelson Mandela was establishing himself as a young lawyer in Johannesburg even as the iron bars of apartheid descended upon his people. Everywhere he looked, he saw a nation spiraling further and further into division, tyranny and injustice. Millions of native blacks—denied education, decent wages and opportunity—were being corralled in townships and Bantustans, passing into the wealthy white areas of the nation as strangers in a strange land. Buses and trains, restrooms and beaches, water fountains and stores were all ruthlessly segregated. When activist leader Mandela was arrested on charges of treason in 1956, he discovered, as he later wrote, that "even treason was not color-blind." The bail for his release was £25, reflecting the perceived insignificance of his people; his white colleague Joe Slovo paid a bail of £250.

Apartheid even stained religion: adherents in the Dutch Reformed Church proudly asserted that the policy reflected God's intentions as well as man's. As TIME reported in 1961 in a story on

Rough justice *In the 1950s, South Africa's white policemen routinely used whiplike* sjamboks *to keep blacks in their place; above, an officer uses a* sjambok *to drive a protester away from a courtroom where other black women were being tried for refusing to carry passbooks, as required under the harsh new strictures of apartheid*

some whites' growing opposition to the system: "South Africa's brutal policy of apartheid, carried out by Christians in the name of Christianity, has long been a challenge to the Christian conscience. Afrikaners traditionally see themselves as the Children of Israel in a Promised Land where God put the black man to serve Him by serving the whites, hewing wood and drawing water."

Under apartheid, South Africa was trapped in a vicious, self-perpetuating cycle of misery: blacks were socially engineered to be inferior by whites, who then viewed the squalor of the ghettos into which they consigned their fellow citizens as convincing proof of their God-given inferiority. As the barriers between the races grew higher, as protests grew louder, as policemen grew edgier, as jails filled up with the best and brightest of the country's blacks, as distrust gave way to hatred and hatred to rage, the nation was on a suicide course. South Africa was a runaway train careering toward a racial bloodbath—but the ruling whites didn't seem to care, so long as blacks were barred from the club car. Someone had to stop the madness. But who?

Mandela, age 19

Troublemaker Of the Transkei

■■■■■

E WAS BORN TO RULE, AND HE WAS CHRISTENED TO BREAK THE rules. Rolihlahla Mandela was born in South Africa's Transkei region on July 18, 1918. It was a notable birth, for he was the great-grandson of Ngubengcuka, a legendary king of the Thembu branch of the Xhosa tribe, and the son of Henry Mandela, a counselor to the presiding Thembu regent Jongintaba Dalindyebo. The boy inherited pride, dignity and a regal bearing from his kingly ancestor and single-minded stubbornness from his father: the year after Rolihlahla was born, Henry refused a local white official's order to appear and explain himself in a dispute over some livestock, and he lost his position. Perhaps Henry hoped his son would be equally resolute: the name Rolihlahla means "Troublemaker." At the age of 7, the boy received the name by which the wider world would come to know him, Nelson; it was bestowed by a British missionary schoolteacher.

The circumstances of his birth would shape the young man's future. He was born a patrician, but he was a nobleman of a diminished realm, for his land was ruled not by his own people but by descendants of white Dutch and British colonists. Within Mandela's lifetime those Europeans would enshrine their racist attitudes in South African law, creating a vicious police state in which a tiny minority of whites held firm sway over a huge majority of poor, deliberately undereducated native black peoples.

It was the destiny of this noble rebel to end these injustices and bring unity to his fractured land. Remarkably, he would do so despite being jailed as a political prisoner for 27 years. Moreover, the revolution he led was not simply political but deeply moral as well, for it resulted not in the rule of one race over another, but in the creation of a new nation in which citizens of all races were treated with equal dignity.

LEADER AND REBEL

For a boy whose name evokes mischief, Mandela's early years were remarkably untroubled. He was born into a large family; his mother Nosekeni Fanny was the third of his father's four wives, and Rolihlahla had 12 siblings. Much later, he would lovingly recall the traditional way of life into which he was born: roaming the veld, playing with his friends and herding sheep and cows. "It is a place where every stone, every blade of grass, every noise made by insects is part of me," he said years later of Qunu, the village in which he grew up.

This idyll was interrupted when Mandela was 9 years old: his father died of lung disease, leaving his son in the care of his close friend Jongintaba, the Thembu tribal regent. Jongintaba was determined that the boy, now called Nelson, would be the first in his family to receive a European-style education. Yet the young man's schooling in leadership began even before he left for the élite boarding school operated by Methodist missionaries in which his powerful patron enrolled him. Listening in on the debates of the tribal council, Mandela learned that Jongintaba led his people the way a shepherd leads his sheep: "He stays behind the flock, letting the most nimble go out ahead, whereupon the others follow, not realizing that all along they are being directed from behind." He also learned the injustices of South Africa's history: "I listened to the elders of the tribe as they related stories of the old days when we ran our own country, governed ourselves, and the heroes that we had when there was a conflict between white and black."

Attending a succession of missionary schools, Mandela acquired some of the values of his teachers, including a puritanical streak that would lead to a lifelong disapproval of excessive drinking and profane speech. He developed a love for intellectual rigor as well, excelling at a lawyer's or philosopher's ability to boil down complex arguments into first principles.

By 1939, Mandela was enrolled in the South African Native College at Fort Hare—the only university in South Africa that admitted blacks. Its campus was the hothouse for an emerging intellectual élite of black South Africans, breeding political, intellectual and moral leaders who in the years to come would march at the head of the struggle against apartheid.

Such matters didn't trouble the young Nelson Mandela, who had thus far developed little political awareness. He had never heard of the African National Congress (A.N.C.) before coming to Fort Hare, where several of the group's founders were on the faculty. He was even largely oblivious of events abroad as World War II drew near. "Neither war nor politics were my concern," Mandela would later say of his Fort Hare years. His dreams were conventional:

Home *Rolihlahla Mandela grew up in South Africa's verdant and mountainous Transkei region—literally, the land beyond the Kei River—in the nation's Eastern Cape region, where his Xhosa people have long been a major tribe* he hoped to work as either a civil servant or an interpreter and counselor in the royal Thembu court, positions that would have brought him financial security, influence and prestige.

Yet Mandela's nature was still in part rebellious, and that would put an end to his university days. When he learned that students at a nearby white college were being fed much better than the blacks at Fort Hare, he organized and led a series of demonstrations. "I was beginning to realize that a black man did not have to accept the dozens of petty indignities directed at him each day," Mandela wrote later of this first small step toward resistance.

He was elected to the student council but refused to take his seat when he learned that a majority of students had declined to vote, in symbolic protest. That gesture could not be tolerated by the school's white overseers, and he was expelled. After he returned home, Jongintaba ordered him to apologize to Fort Hare's administrators and return to school. Mandela refused, then dug in his heels further when the regent arranged for his ward to marry a woman for whom the young man felt no attraction. Defying the authority of both his school and his patron, he seized control of his destiny and fled to Johannesburg in April 1941.

CITY LIGHTS

Nelson Mandela, now 22, was many things by this point—intelligent, proud and a natural leader—but sophisticated he was not. Exposure to the cosmopolitan whirl of South Africa's "City of Gold" opened Mandela's eyes. The booming wartime economy had remade Johannesburg into a lively, multiracial metropolis, where a thriving community of musicians, writers and artists was giving South Africa's black culture a fresh, strong voice. The government, desperate to fill factories running full-tilt and eager to avoid political trouble during wartime, had temporarily stopped enforcing such antiblack measures as pass laws and internal travel restrictions, bolstering the sense that a new age was dawning.

Mandela soon learned how relentlessly grim life could be for urban blacks. Finding a job as a mine policeman, he saw firsthand the appalling conditions under which native "boys" worked to enrich their white masters. White companies "became wealthy beyond the dreams of Croesus," Mandela observed, while poorly paid Africans were brutalized by mine police and housed, segregated by tribe, in wretched barracks. Mandela was fired from his job after his managers (who maintained close ties with cooperative tribal chiefs who supplied cheap, docile workers) learned that he had come to Johannesburg in defiance of Jongintaba.

Looking for work, Mandela soon made the acquaintance of Walter Sisulu, a real estate agent who was the son of a white father and black mother. A rebel in a business suit, Sisulu was both successful and seditious, the perfect mentor for a young man who was increasingly convinced that he was born to lead but not yet certain of where and how. "The moment I met him, I knew that this is the man I need," Sisulu would later recall of Mandela. "When he came into my office, I marked him at once as a man with great qualities who was destined to play an important part." On Sisulu's recommendation, Mandela was hired as a clerk in the law firm of Witkin, Sidelsky & Eidelman. Mandela later called Lazar Sidelsky, a partner in the firm who took the aspiring lawyer under his wing, "the first white man who treated me as a human being." By 1943, Mandela was studying law at the University of the Witwatersrand.

In addition to working and studying full-time, Mandela now became more involved in politics. That same year, he took a leading role in helping to organize a city bus boycott in reaction to a draconian fare hike that hit low-earning blacks hard. After nine days of running

Differences Doom a Marriage

Nelson Mandela's first wife was a hometown girl, Transkei native Evelyn Ntoko Mase. The two met in Johannesburg in 1943, where Evelyn was working as a nurse; they were introduced by Walter Sisulu, the anti-apartheid activist who was Mandela's mentor and Evelyn's cousin. Mandela, then 25 and working as a law clerk while beginning his legal studies at the University of the Witwatersrand, was ready to start a family. The two settled down in a three-room house in the Orlando district of Soweto, the black township on the outskirts of Johannesburg. Their son Thembi was born about a year after the 1944 wedding; a daughter, Makaziwe, was born in 1947, but she was a frail infant who died at the age of 9 months.

Nelson and Evelyn were initially seen as a model couple; Evelyn's female friends admired Mandela, who was willing to help out with chores around the house at a time when few African men did so. But the strain of Mandela's political activism began taking a toll on the marriage, as meetings and protests kept him away from home. Evelyn was also changing; always a religious person, she became increasingly involved in her Jehovah's Witnesses denomination, which stressed a spiritual rather than a political approach to life.

The arrival of a second son, Makgatho, in 1950 and daughter Makaziwe (named for her deceased sister) in 1954 did not salvage the marriage. When Mandela was first arrested for treason in 1956, he returned home after being bailed out of jail to find a bare house: Evelyn had decamped to live with her brother. The two officially divorced in 1957. Evelyn died of respiratory failure in Johannesburg in 2004; Mandela saluted her in his autobiography as "a very good woman, charming, strong, and faithful, and a fine mother."

41

Athlete *Mandela spars with champion boxer Jerry Moloi in 1957; the young lawyer loved the sport but admitted he never excelled at it. His lifelong devotion to exercise helped him keep fit and healthy during his long prison years*

empty buses, the line's operators gave in and restored fares to the old price. That marked Mandela's first political victory, as well as his first involvement with the A.N.C.—at the time a largely moribund organization that counseled endless patience in the face of repression.

AN EMERGING RADICAL

With his appetite for political action whetted, Mandela allied himself with a Zulu militant and lawyer, Anton Lembede, who was leading a push for a new youth wing within the A.N.C. in hopes of sparking more actions like the successful bus boycott. Lembede unapologetically disdained "the worship and idolization of European men and ideas" and led Mandela to view his own career in a new light. His college education and legal training in the atmosphere of British paternalism had tempted him, he now came to believe, to be drawn into a white-sanctioned black élite that would help validate white colonialism. "Like Lembede, I came to see the antidote as militant African nationalism," he later recalled.

By April 1944, the upstarts had established the Youth League over the objections of the A.N.C.'s entrenched leadership. Lembede was president; the executive committee included Mandela, Sisulu and Mandela's Fort Hare college friend Oliver Tambo, a lawyer and Sisulu protégé. They issued a statement declaring that the African native "now elects to determine his future by his own efforts."

Many advocates of black liberation among Mandela's generation had imagined that

Defender *Mandela speaks to a group of 21 women who were being tried for creating a public disturbance after they took part in a protest march to oppose the passage of the Bantu education laws in 1955*

World War II would bring lasting change, forcing the government to move toward moderation and inclusion. But when the crisis atmosphere passed, the white regime backed away from its conciliatory measures. The turning point came in August 1946, when miners went on strike for better working conditions. The strike was broken when nine black miners were bayonetted to death, discrediting the patient restraint preached by the Old Guard among the A.N.C.'s leadership. Within weeks, the sense of foreboding was reinforced by new racial laws that forbade the sale of land to Indians. The harsh new trend became more pronounced with the election of 1948, in which the National Party and Afrikaner Party formed a coalition, took control of the government and began writing apartheid into the nation's constitution.

PROGRESS ROLLED BACK

As the situation became grimmer, Mandela's resolve grew firmer. He became secretary of the A.N.C.'s Youth League in 1947, after Lembede's sudden death. In 1949 he, Sisulu and Tambo acted as kingmakers and ushered Dr. James Moroka, an advocate for militant mass action and boycotts, into the presidency of the A.N.C. Mandela's stature grew with each step. By 1950 he had completed his legal apprenticeship and was a practicing lawyer. In partnership with Tambo, he now opened South Africa's first black law firm. With an endless roster of black clients who had nowhere else to turn for help in fighting the injustices of apartheid, their business thrived. "Phone Mandela and Tambo!" became a familiar refrain among blacks who were arrested when police broke up meetings of militant organizations, and the two young lawyers also became the A.N.C.'s official legal counsel.

Mandela now seemed to spend as much time in the streets as in the courtroom. At May Day protests in 1950, he watched policemen massacre 19 peaceful demonstrators, and he narrowly escaped being killed. "That day was a turning point in my life," he would later recall. A month later, Mandela took the lead in organizing a national "Day of Mourning" protest, and he was elected president of the A.N.C.'s Youth League shortly afterward. At the 35th annual A.N.C. congress in December 1951, Mandela joined those calling for a Defiance Campaign of boycotts and passive resistance if the government refused to repeal six unjust laws that were at the heart of apartheid's legal structure. The campaign resulted in more than 8,000 arrests, including Mandela, who saw the inside of a jail cell for the first time that year.

IN THE VANGUARD

Prosperous and resolute, intelligent and widely respected, Mandela cut a reassuring, even dashing figure amid increasingly desperate times. He had now acquired the sophistication he lacked upon arriving in Johannesburg a decade earlier. He also was developing an unmistakable air of authority, based in part on his stern self-discipline. Rising each day before dawn to work out in a boxing gym, Mandela would work late into each night, trying to use the letter of South Africa's law to subvert its goal of racial discrimination.

As his political reach broadened, Mandela began working with Indians, coloureds and others cast out under apartheid's strict racial codes. These new alliances helped expand his political thinking in a critical way: while many black radicals envisioned an all-black future for South Africa, Mandela became convinced that the liberation movement had to include everyone—blacks, Indians, coloureds and whites, as well as members of all the nation's tribes.

In August 1953, Z.K. Matthews, one of Mandela's professors at Fort Hare, proposed "a national convention ... to draw up a Freedom Charter for the democratic South Africa of the future." Its centerpiece was the principle of one vote for one adult, regardless of race, tribe or ethnicity. Mandela embraced the plan, which rebuked both emerging black nationalists who hated whites and the white government. He would hew to the charter's radically inclusive vision of South Africa's racial future throughout his political career, often at great cost.

In its final draft, the Freedom Charter began with words that echoed the founding documents of the U.S., the ideals of the French Revolution and the United Nations Universal Declaration of Human Rights: "We, the people of South Africa declare for all our country and the world to know: That South Africa belongs to all who live in it , black and white, and that no government can claim just authority unless it is based on the will of the people." It would take Mandela and the A.N.C. four decades to see those ideas enshrined in law.

The A.N.C. attempted to vote on the Freedom Charter at a Congress of the People, which convened at Kliptown, outside Johannesburg, on June 26, 1955. But before the roll of more than 3,000 delegates could be called, police shut down the meeting and arrested many of the participants. The charter would not be ratified until April 1956. Although Mandela was not arrested, he was by now recognized by the government as an important radical leader and was legally banned from making speeches or attending meetings of any kind. He lingered at the outskirts of the Kliptown congress, wearing a disguise. The young Thembu nobleman who had been dubbed "Troublemaker" at birth was beginning to live up to his name.

GAMMA

Dressed for success *Tall, well tailored and regal in bearing, Mandela—seen here as a young lawyer in Johannesburg in the 1950s— never lost the aristocratic posture that was his birthright as a Xhosa nobleman. His love of fine tailoring, which he was unable to indulge during his long years in prison, was one of his few personal foibles, and friends teased him about it*

Influences

Throughout his career as an activist, Nelson Mandela was inspired by other 20th century leaders, and through his changing heroes, we can trace the arc of his political evolution. As a young man he admired the nonviolent political strategies of Mohandas Gandhi and Martin Luther King Jr., but when he decided their methods were futile in South Africa, he turned to more militant figures for role models: African nationalists and guerrilla warriors such as Mao Zedong and Fidel Castro.

Mohandas Gandhi: 1869-1948

"Both Gandhi and I suffered colonial oppression," Mandela wrote for TIME in 1999, "and both of us mobilized our peoples against governments that violated our freedoms." Calling Gandhi, who spent more than 20 years in South Africa and first developed his philosophy of non-violent resistance there, "the archetypal anticolonial revolutionary," Mandela clarified the similarities and differences between his movement and Gandhi's. He praised Gandhi's "strategy of noncooperation, his assertion that we can be dominated only if we cooperate with our dominators." But he also observed that "Gandhi remained committed to nonviolence; I followed the Gandhian strategy for as long as I could, but then there came a point in our struggle when the brute force of the oppressor could no longer be countered through passive resistance alone. We … added a military dimension to our struggle. Even then, we chose sabotage because it did not involve the loss of life, and it offered the best hope for future race relations." Still, the words Mandela wrote in TIME about Gandhi could apply equally well to their author: "His inner resilience overpowered him with a sense of mission … to redeem the dignity of the racially exploited, to pave the way for the liberation of the colonized the world over and to develop a blueprint for a new social order."

Joe Louis: 1914-1981

"As a young man, I idolized the Brown Bomber, Joe Louis, who took on not only his opponents in the ring but racists outside of it," Mandela wrote in his autobiography. Of his own brief career as an amateur boxer in Soweto during the 1950s, Mandela was less proud: "I had neither enough power to compensate for my lack of speed, nor enough speed to make up for my lack of power." In his 30s, Mandela bore more than a passing resemblance to Louis and he grew up feeling an enormous sense of personal vindication that his hero came back in 1938, after an initial defeat, to pummel German champion Max Schmeling (who was at the time widely perceived as a Nazi and supporter of Aryan supremacy, though he was neither). At left, Louis lands a punch on Lou Nova at Yankee Stadium in 1941.

In 2003, the former amateur boxer from Soweto joined his boyhood hero as a member of the World Boxing Hall of Fame. The citation referred to Mandela as "the greatest champion of all time" for having "knocked out apartheid."

Winston Churchill: 1874-1965

Churchill, the defiant champion of empire, may seem an odd hero for Mandela, colonialism's great foe. Yet Mandela loved Churchill's courage, his fire, his eloquence. "Never give in," Churchill declared, "never yield to force; never yield to the apparently overwhelming might of the enemy." These words helped steel Mandela's resolve in prison. Churchill's willingness to form alliances with those whose policies he hated, as he did with Stalin, also influenced Mandela in dealing both with rival black leaders and with the heads of the apartheid state. In particular, Mandela loved a newsreel image of Churchill weeping over a lost ship in World War II; it proved, he said, that leaders can show emotion in public.

Kwame Nkrumah: 1909-1972

"In my country," Mandela wrote in his autobiography, "we go to prison first and then become President." But South Africa is not unique in this respect, as the life of Kwame Nkrumah shows. Born in the village of Nkroful in the British colony of Gold Coast, he was educated in the U.S., then returned home in 1947 to lead the fight for freedom. Jailed by the British for sedition, he was elected the country's leader in 1951, while still in jail. As a result, the British abandoned the Gold Coast and nearby Togoland. Both former colonies were incorporated into the new nation of Ghana, with Nkrumah as its first Prime Minister and President.

Martin Luther King Jr.: 1929-1968

The United States and South Africa share parallel histories in some ways: both nations were settled by the Dutch, conquered by the British, fought for their independence—and created societies wracked by enduring racial tension. Mandela always cited U.S. civil rights leader King as an enduring influence.

If Mandela absorbed pacifism primarily from Gandhi (and later rejected it as ineffectual in his particular circumstances), he and his colleagues in the A.N.C. learned from King the power to mobilize world opinion through the media. The careers of both King and Mandela offer object lessons in how an unjustly jailed leader can transform a political cause into a moral crusade—although Mandela would spend decades in prison, compared with the relatively short periods during which King was incarcerated in Birmingham, Ala. (left), and elsewhere. Mandela points out in his autobiography, however, the essential ways in which his struggle in South Africa differed from that of King in America: "The United States was a democracy with constitutional guarantees of equal rights that protected nonviolent protest (though there was still prejudice against blacks); South Africa was a police state with a constitution that enshrined inequality and an army that responded to nonviolence with force."

Jawaharlal P. Nehru: 1889-1964

India's Prime Minister earned Mandela's enduring respect in the 1950s, when India became the first nation to protest apartheid by imposing economic sanctions on South Africa. Mandela's biographer Anthony Sampson argues that Mandela came to respect Nehru, the tough, hard-nosed politician, more than the saintly, turn-the-other-cheek Gandhi. In the mid-1950s, at a time when South Africa's white leaders played the nation's races against each other, Mandela reached out to South Africa's large population of Indians, forging bonds that would endure—and that pointed the way to a multiracial future.

Gamal Abdel Nasser: 1918-1970

For Arabs of Africa and the Middle East in the 1950s and '60s, the President of Egypt filled the role that Nelson Mandela would later occupy for Africa's blacks: he was a unifying figure whose charisma spilled across borders. Nasser's pan-Arabist ideology was a heady mix of nationalism, anticolonialism and socialism that informed the political theories of the African National Congress for decades. As Mandela wrote in *Long Walk to Freedom*, "Egypt was an important model for us, for we could witness first-hand the program of socialist economic reform being launched by President Nasser ... Many of these reforms were precisely the sort of things we in the A.N.C. someday hoped to enact."

FROM TOP: GENE HERRICK—AP IMAGES; PIX INC.—TIME LIFE PICTURES; AP IMAGES

Mao Zedong: 1893-1976

When Mandela assumed leadership of the Umkhonto We Sizwe wing of the A.N.C., he took up the study of successful armed resistance movements around the world in the 20th century. Responsible for raising a guerrilla army, learning military strategy and developing tactics, South Africa's "Black Pimpernel" was heavily influenced by the success of Mao's communist revolution in China, which brought him to power in 1949 and was still fresh news in the 1950s. Mandela would later recall learning from "Edgar Snow's brilliant *Red Star over China* … that it was Mao's determination and non-traditional thinking that led him to victory."

Mandela was confined in prison when Mao's star fell after his death in 1976. It was only after the Chinese leader's demise that full accounts of the terrors of his brutal reign over a sequestered communist China were finally revealed for all the world to see—and Snow's worshipful biography was discredited.

Ahmed Ben Bella: 1918-2012

Like Kwame Nkrumah, Ben Bella was an anticolonial liberator who would chart the path followed by Mandela: he went from prison to the presidency in becoming the first leader of a free Algeria. During the nation's fight for independence, the French air force intercepted rebel leader Ben Bella's plane in 1956 and diverted it to France. Ben Bella was jailed on an island until he was released in 1962, after he was elected Algeria's leader while still incarcerated. Mandela, then a rebel in hiding, slipped out of South Africa to attend the triumphal 1962 parade at which Ben Bella's guerrilla fighters marched before their leader before his inauguration. "Enthusiasm simply bewildering," Mandela wrote in his diary. Ben Bella joined his mentor, Egypt's Nasser, in funneling covert support to the A.N.C. and once weighed sending his army to topple the apartheid regime—a plan that was scotched by a 1965 coup that removed Ben Bella from office and drove him into exile.

Fidel Castro: 1926-

A charismatic David to the West's Goliath, the Cuban was an inspiration to Mandela, who admired Castro's rhetoric: the famous "history will absolve me" speech Castro gave at his 1953 trial inspired Mandela's "it is an ideal for which I am prepared to die" oration at the Rivonia Trial. Mandela modeled the A.N.C.'s acts of insurgency in part on Castro's guerrilla campaigns, and he welcomed Castro's 1975 decision to send troops to Angola to counter opposition forces supported by the South African government. But Mandela may have viewed the Cuban strongman's career as a cautionary tale: unlike Castro (and Mao Zedong), Mandela remained a servant of his people, rather than their master.

The Years of Living Dangerously

■■ ■■■

WITH THE 1956 RATIFICATION OF THE FREEDOM CHARTER, the African National Congress offered South Africans riven by race a vision of a new future. Soaring in its rhetoric and egalitarian in its philosophy, the manifesto imagined a new nation, conceived in liberty and dedicated to the proposition that all men are created equal. But the years that followed its adoption underscored the extent of the racial fanaticism codified in apartheid and measured the distance between the A.N.C.'s dreams and the reality of life in South Africa's grim black townships. The Freedom Charter ushered in a decade of bloodshed during which the foes of apartheid were plagued by factional schisms even as the iron grip of racial tyranny tightened around them.

In the midst of this maelstrom was Nelson Mandela, who, like his country, would undergo a profound evolution in the years between 1956 and 1964. In the early 1950s he was a philosophical, nonviolent resister of racial oppression whose weapons were words and whose battlefield was a courtroom. But in the space of a few years, he would undergo a radical transformation: the respectable, prosperous and law-abiding Johannesburg attorney with a tranquil domestic life would become an insolvent debtor, abandoned by his first wife, who lived underground in disguise as a wanted man while conspiring with like-minded revolutionaries to plot sabotage against his nation's government.

Mandela's transformation into a fugitive guerrilla began even before the ratification of the Freedom Charter, as South Africa's government passed new laws that steadily expanded the long reach of its racial policies. The linchpin of the Afrikaner-dominated Parliament's grave new world was the policy dubbed "grand apartheid" by Minister of Native Affairs Hendrik Verwoerd, who would become Prime Minister in 1958. "Verwoerd's grim plot," as Mandela called it, created an elaborate new legal apparatus to enforce complete separation of the races.

Previously, segregation had largely been an improvised affair in South Africa, similar to

MAYIBUYE ARCHIVES

Boiling Point *Shortly after the Sharpeville Massacre on March 21, 1960, a grinning Mandela defied the apartheid regime by publicly consigning his passbook—the foremost symbol of the exclusionary racist policies of the government—to the flames*

the unwritten Jim Crow laws that helped keep much of the U.S. effectively segregated for 100 years after the Civil War. Although brutal, unjust and humiliating, segregation in South Africa had long been haphazard and inconsistent. Verwoerd planned to get it right this time. Black South Africans would be evacuated at gunpoint from lands they had occupied for centuries and herded into tribal Bantustans, where their only economic function would be to provide cheap labor for South Africa's white-dominated economy. Schooling of blacks would be legally prohibited, to prevent "the wrong type of education" (in Verwoerd's phrase) from incubating more troublemakers like Mandela and his allies.

As the tentacles of apartheid wove themselves more inextricably into South African life, the government began a wide-ranging treason investigation. For Mandela, the knock on the door came at dawn on Dec. 5, 1956. When he answered, the attorney and activist was confronted by a squad of police officers holding a warrant for his arrest. At the same time, 155 other suspects were taken into custody.

Thus began the marathon Treason Trial, an ordeal that would destroy Mandela's already strained marriage to Evelyn Mase, dry up his law practice and drain his finances. The trial, which ended in 1961 with not one of the 156 original defendants convicted, created two unintended consequences: it was farcical theater, a showcase for the ineptitude of the nation's security services; and it became a venue for uniting antiapartheid leaders at a time when most had been legally banned from meeting with one another for several years.

NEW RIVALS

This newfound unity proved crucial, because a threat that Mandela took far more seriously than the absurdism of the Treason Trial emerged at the same time. Several factions of black nationalists, who rejected the A.N.C. policy that the nation's future should include all races as well as blacks, formed splinter organizations and began bidding to lead the fight against racial oppression that had once been the exclusive province of the A.N.C.

Mandela's view of black nationalism changed slowly over time. At the start of his career as an activist, he would later recall, "I was angry at the white man, not at racism." He later acknowledged that during this period, "I believed that it was an undiluted African nationalism, not Marxism or multiracialism, that would liberate us." By the mid-1950s, however, Mandela had come to believe the opposite: that a racially inclusive vision of South Africa's future was the only one that could overcome apartheid and heal the nation's wounds.

Chief among the groups that disagreed with this vision was the Pan-Africanist Congress (P.A.C.), founded in 1959 by Robert Sobukwe, a charismatic, scholarly man six years younger than Mandela, and his equal in distinguished bearing. The P.A.C. leader—tall, handsome and eloquent—projected an aura of immense strength. His new party appealed to the A.N.C.'s domestic base and competed with the older group for support from abroad. Moreover, while the A.N.C. leadership included avowed Marxists, the P.A.C. was dogmatically anticommunist. Foes of apartheid in Europe and the U.S. could now consider diverting their financial contributions to the P.A.C. "Because of the P.A.C.'s anticommunism," Mandela wrote years later, "they became the darlings of the Western press and the American State Department"

During the decades-long fight against apartheid, the A.N.C.'s cooperation with avowed communists would put the group at odds with Britain, the U.S. and other anti-Soviet nations. As a young man, Mandela considered communism a white European ideology,

Treason trial *Above left, Mandela joins fellow defendants as they are bused to a Pretoria courtroom in 1956 during the Treason Trial, which lasted for five years. At right, some of the 156 defendants placed on trial for advocating treason against the apartheid regime pose for a picture. At bottom, protesters march in the streets on May 19, 1956, the first day of the trial. Some 5,000 blacks waited in line for entry to the hall, while others carried signs of support for leaders of the antiapartheid movement*

and he helped disrupt meetings of the South African Communist Party (S.A.C.P.). Later he became convinced that many white communists, such as his close friend Joe Slovo, were genuinely committed to ending apartheid. Pointing out that for many years the only whites in South Africa who supported the A.N.C. cause were communists, Mandela viewed the A.N.C.-S.A.C.P. alliance as a marriage of convenience, and he insisted that he and other A.N.C. leaders were not party members. He noted that both the U.S. and Britain allied themselves with the U.S.S.R. to fight a common foe during World War II, despite their hatred of Soviet communism. "The cynical have always suggested that the communists were using us," he wrote later. "But who is to say that we were not using them?"

That dynamic was seized upon by the white government of South Africa, eager to cut off foreign support for the A.N.C. and find friends of its own abroad. In 1950, the apartheid regime passed the Suppression of Communism Act, which made it a crime to advocate any doctrine that promoted "political, industrial, social or economic change within the Union by the promotion of disturbance or disorder." The law had little to do with communism per se but made for brilliant political branding: now anyone who opposed apartheid could be cast to foreign eyes as a communist. The tactic proved highly successful, garnering support for South Africa's regime from Britain and the U.S. through decades of the cold war, in spite of the African nation's increasingly squalid apartheid policies.

Massacre at Sharpeville

Even as he embraced communists as allies in the 1950s, Mandela began to reconsider the effectiveness of nonviolence as a political tool. He had always admired Mohandas Gandhi, who employed the tactic of passive resistance to help liberate India from British control. But Mandela gradually concluded that the armed force employed by the South African government to uphold apartheid far surpassed the measures used by the British in India. "For me," Mandela wrote in his autobiography, "nonviolence was not a moral principle but a strategy; there is no moral goodness in using an ineffective weapon." Mandela was among the first A.N.C. leaders to consider abandoning peaceful civil disobedience, but his growing advocacy of violence was long dismissed by the older A.N.C. leaders.

The belief that force would have to be met with force, along with the concern that the initiative was passing from the A.N.C. to rival groups, received grim confirmation in 1960, while the plodding Treason Trial was still in session. On March 21, the P.A.C. led a demonstration against the much hated passbook laws, which required black South Africans to show domestic travel permits whenever they ventured outside one of the Bantustans. As protesters gathered outside a police station in the township of Sharpeville, south of Johannesburg, jumpy police officers panicked, fired into the unarmed crowd—and kept firing.

The death toll for the Sharpeville Massacre was 69, with more than 180 others wounded. The event proved a watershed for the already distressed nation. In the wake of the massacre, the government imposed a state of emergency, banned the A.N.C. and other antiapartheid groups and arrested the regime's opponents by the thousands. In an act of public defiance that gave voice to his increasing radicalization, Mandela publicly burned his own passbook. The massacre also brought the world's attention to the inequities of South Africa's brutal system: both the U.S. State Department and the United Nations strongly protested the white regime's actions and the entire system of apartheid.

In this context, the 1961 not-guilty verdict for Mandela in the Treason Trial was anticlimactic, if welcome. The A.N.C. leadership was now persuaded by Mandela's calls for the use of limited violence that would be tightly focused on government facilities rather than citizens. As always, Mandela took a very long view, later noting, "We chose sabotage because it did not involve the loss of life, and it offered the best hope for future race relations."

SPEAR OF THE NATION

Shortly after the Treason Trial ended, Mandela was secretly chosen to lead a new wing of the A.N.C., to be known as Umkhonto we Sizwe (Spear of the Nation, often abbreviated as M.K.). Around this time, Mandela made what would be his last public appearance for almost 30 years at an A.N.C. conference in Pietermaritzburg, where he again proposed a new, nonracial constitution for South Africa. The government immediately issued a warrant for his arrest, and Mandela disappeared into hiding to raise a guerrilla army. Within six months, the Spear of the Nation made its debut with a series of after-hours bombings of government offices.

Mandela had been preparing for life as a fugitive for some time. Midway through the Treason Trial, anticipating that the A.N.C. would soon be officially banned, he had proposed organizing the group into secret cells. Now the entire A.N.C. began functioning as a secret network, and Mandela began his life on the lam. Soon dubbed "the Black Pimpernel" by reporters, Mandela the fugitive captured the imagination of South Africans opposed to

Enter Winnie

"I can not say for certain if there is such a thing as love at first sight," Nelson Mandela reminisced in his autobiography, *Long Walk to Freedom*. "But I do know that the moment I first glimpsed Winnie Nomzamo, I knew that I wanted to have her as my wife."

Mandela caught that first glimpse at a Johannesburg bus stop in 1957. Years later, neither would say whether it was by coincidence or design that she walked into his law office the next day. She was a social worker, barely 20 years old, born in the Transkei, like Mandela and his first wife Evelyn. Already a respected leader in the fight against apartheid, Mandela was almost twice Winnie's age and had a wife and three children.

But as Mandela's first marriage ended amid the early days of the Treason Trial, the emerging statesman and the wide-eyed beauty became the A.N.C.'s glamour couple. They married in 1957, within a year of meeting (ever the tribal traditionalist, Mandela paid a dowry to his bride's family in cattle), but the two were almost immediately separated by events. Mandela devoted most of the next few years to traveling and organizing for the A.N.C., then spent several years after that underground, as a wanted fugitive. In spite of this, their union managed to produce two daughters, Zendiziswa and Zenani, but Mandela was away so frequently and for so long that one of them once asked Winnie, "Where does Daddy live?"

Then came the Rivonia Trial verdict and decades during which the couple saw each other only through a glass partition on Robben Island. Winnie would later write that when she married Mandela, she knew she was marrying the movement he led. As she would admit years later, "I never knew him ...To me, he represented a symbol of resistance."

On the run *Protesters flee shots fired by policemen during the March 1960 Sharpeville Massacre, a turning point in the history of apartheid in South Africa, in which 69 demonstrators were murdered in cold blood and hundreds more were injured*

apartheid, regardless of race. Often disguised as a chauffeur or "garden boy," he eluded a nationwide manhunt, then took a guerrilla's grand tour of Africa, seeking support. At a time when black Africans were shaking off their colonial ties, Mandela, in his new role as a South African Che Guevara, found a host of sympathizers and more than a few mentors. Mandela had once embodied an incongruous combination of tribal prince, Johannesburg lawyer and social activist. But this partitioned identity now gave way to a less conflicted persona—that of a guerrilla outlaw and charismatic, elusive, invisible legend.

Returning to South Africa early in 1962, Mandela was finally arrested in August, pulled over by police on a motorway while riding at high speed from Durban to Johannesburg. (It has long been rumored, but never confirmed, that South African security forces were tipped off to his whereabouts by the U.S. C.I.A.). He was put in jail to await trial, and the police apprehended many of the rest of the members of the A.N.C. high command eleven months later, on July 11, 1963, at their rural hideout, Liliesleaf Farm in Rivonia, outside Johannesburg.

Shortly after Mandela's arrest, South African law was amended to eliminate habeas corpus protections, making it legal for the government to imprison anyone suspected of a "political crime." Mandela was initially charged with traveling without a passport and inciting strikes, for which he was quickly convicted and sentenced to five years. Prosecutors now used the new, looser legal standards to charge Mandela and nine co-defendants from the Rivonia farm with sabotage and conspiracy to overthrow the government. The 221 counts

against the men included a detailed description of Operation Mayibuye, a grandiose, foolhardy scheme for revolution that called for M.K. to establish guerrilla camps across South Africa and prepare for an invasion by A.N.C. fighters in exile that would include air support and submarines.

Mandela and his colleagues refused to contest the charges, a momentous decision considering that the prosecution was seeking the death penalty. Rather, they determined to use the trial as a bully pulpit to bear witness to the moral legitimacy of their struggle. "I do not ... deny that I planned sabotage," Mandela told the court. But he described his deeds as the "result of a calm and sober assessment of the political situation that had arisen after many years of tyranny, exploitation, and oppression of my people by the whites."

Verwoerd, by now Prime Minister, begged to differ. "These people are criminals—communist criminals—just as any spy caught and executed in the United States," he argued. But Mandela insisted that he worked with communists and made no apology for it, but was not one himself. He concluded his statement to the court with a burst of stirring oratory that would smolder for decades in the shacks and shebeens, huts and hovels of South Africa's oppressed, even as it burned in the conscience of the white world: "During my lifetime I have dedicated myself to the struggle of the African people. I have fought against white domination, and I have fought against black domination. I have cherished the ideal of a democratic and free society in which all persons live together in harmony and with equal opportunities. It

WARWICK ROBINSON

Apartheid's harvest *The Sharpeville Massacre raised global awareness of the injustices of South Africa's system of "grand apartheid." At left, policemen survey a street littered with bodies shortly after the massacre in the township some 35 miles south of Johannesburg*

is an ideal which I hope to live for and to achieve. But, if needs be, it is an ideal for which I am prepared to die."

With his resonant voice and imposing presence, Mandela occupied the moral center of gravity of the Rivonia Trial. He had at last grown into the leader that for decades he had seemed to hint he could be. The tragic irony was that he had fully blossomed in what seemed sure to be the last weeks of his life—too late to accomplish the great work for which he seemed destined, the unification of his nation.

But much to everyone's surprise, including his own, Mandela was not sentenced to death. Instead, when he and the other defendants, as expected, were convicted on all counts, they were all sentenced to life in prison. On the day he began serving his sentence, Nelson Mandela was 44 years old. He would not draw another breath as a free man until he was 71. But during the trying days to come, his reservoir of conviction, resolve and compelling moral authority would only grow deeper, as Mandela was tempered and disciplined by long, bitter years apart from the struggle he now believed he was born to lead.

The Black Pimpernel

"The seconds I spent waiting for the light to change seemed like hours," Nelson Mandela later recalled of a close call during his fugitive days as South Africa's Black Pimpernel. Disguised in workman's coveralls, he had stopped at an intersection when a car pulled up beside him bearing the chief of the local security police—whom Mandela knew well from previous arrests. But the chief never looked his way, the signal turned green, and Mandela remained at large. Another time, when he noticed a black police officer scrutinizing him from a distance, Mandela feared the worst. But as the policeman drew near, he gave Mandela a thumbs-up, whispered "Africa" and walked away.

During his 17 months in hiding, Mandela traveled widely around Africa (and as far away as London) to drum up support for the A.N.C. and its guerrilla war. "For the first time in my life, I was a free man," he later said of his days on the run. In a newly independent Algeria, he received training in the tactics that had driven away the French. In Addis Ababa, where he traveled under a false Ethiopian passport, Mandela spent weeks studying guerrilla tactics under an officer who had fought the Italians in World War II. His introduction to the wider world included history and culture: in Egypt, Mandela admired Gamal Nasser's program of nationalization and also discovered that "Egyptians were creating great works of art and architecture when Europeans were still living in caves."

Going undercover *At left, Mandela speaks at the A.N.C. conference in Pietermaritzburg on March 25, 1961, his last public appearance for 30 years. Later, center, he meets military leaders in Algeria; at right, he views the Thames with British supporters*

African Prince *Mandela, the natty dresser who was almost always seen in a suit during his days as a dignified young lawyer in the 1950s, electrified a Pretoria courtroom in 1962 when he appeared for his first hearing in the Rivonia Trial wearing a traditional Xhosa kaross. "I was literally carrying on my back the history, culture and heritage of my people," he later wrote*

The Prison Years

■▬▬▬▬

PRISON STEELED NELSON MANDELA—WHAT DID NOT KILL HIM MADE HIM stronger. He went to jail on Robben Island in 1964 as a self-described rabble rouser and emerged as what André Malraux once described as that rarest thing in the world: a mature man. Twenty-seven years behind bars formed the leader the world came to admire: thoughtful, measured, controlled, dignified, statesman-like. While the sensitive herdboy from the Transkei never stopped feeling the lash of racism, prison taught him to hide his pain behind a mask of proud indifference. Yet the hard years of imprisonment also converted Mandela's youthful loathing of those who practiced apartheid into a purer, more refined anger against the racist system itself. When he finally walked out of prison, nothing was going to stop him from overturning the order that had kept him behind bars for so many years.

And prison mythologized Mandela. The long years he sacrificed for his beliefs are the central talisman of his legend, the first thing children learn about him, the feat of awe-inspiring endurance and resolve mentioned in the first sentence of his obituaries. The strict isolation in which the South African authorities kept their foremost prisoner—few visitors, no pictures for 25 years—turned him from a living, breathing man into a larger-than-life legend. And that, in retrospect, was essential to the healing of his nation and its development after apartheid. South Africa needed a person who could stand above the fray, speaking for all sides, and Mandela's years in prison made him the only person who could play this vital role.

"Prison and the authorities conspire to rob each man of his dignity," Mandela wrote in his autobiography. "In and of itself, that assured that I would survive, for any man or institution that tries to rob me of my dignity will lose because I will not part with it at any price or under any pressure." This philosophy would maintain Mandela's resolve during years of intense privation. He first demonstrated it in 1963, during the Rivonia Trial, when for the first time he

Captive *This picture of Mandela on Robben Island was published in a London newspaper in 1965. For the photo, he and other political prisoners were put to work sewing, rather than breaking rocks, and were issued clothing of better quality than their normal daily wear. Mandela is wearing the short pants he hated, feeling they were intended to suggest the black prisoners were immature*

Prison yard *This 1965 photo is one of the few pictures of Mandela and his fellow Rivonia Trial inmates on Robben Island. Mandela is believed to be the fifth figure from left in the top row. The close-up photo of Mandela on the previous page was taken on the same occasion*

was briefly held in South Africa's legendary maximum-security prison on Robben Island, in Table Bay near Cape Town. On his first night at the facility, when a young Afrikaner warder made a motion as if to strike him, Mandela drew himself up to his full 6-ft. 2-in. height and declared, "If you so much as lay a hand on me, I will take you to the highest court in the land. And when I finish with you, you will be as poor as a church mouse." The prisoner's demeanor was so commanding—and his reputation as a successful lawyer so well known—that the guard immediately backed down.

REBEL

Early in his life term at Robben Island, Mandela provoked another confrontation, complaining about his prison garb. Black prisoners were issued short pants, while Indians and coloureds were given long pants, and Mandela knew the point was to clothe the blacks as "boys." He loudly demanded long trousers, which arrived two weeks later. "No pinstripe, three-piece suit has ever pleased me as much," he later wrote. But when he learned that he was the only black prisoner to receive the long pants, Mandela refused to put them on.

In Mandela's first years at Robben Island, the days were solitary, poor, nasty, brutish—and long. Although the workday began at 5:30 a.m., the disciplined Mandela arose earlier to conduct his daily exercise regimen, doing sit-ups, push-ups and running in place in his cell; his lifelong devotion to fitness would keep him vigorous well into his 80s. Breakfast was maize porridge accompanied by maize-based "coffee"; lunch was boiled maize; dinner was yet more maize, topped off with a vegetable or, every other night, a gristly piece of meat. The day's work consisted of hammering stones into gravel, and talking between prisoners was forbidden. Lights-out was early in the evening, again with no talking permitted between cells.

In these first, harshest years in jail, visitors were restricted to one family member every six months; personal letters followed the same schedule. Mandela believed this denial of family relationships was one of the single most inhumane aspects of his imprisonment. He eagerly awaited Winnie's visits but found them far too short and, since they were not allowed to touch each other, very frustrating. In 1968 his mother, appearing very frail, came to visit him for the only time during his confinement; she died just weeks later, and Mandela was not permitted to attend her funeral. The next year he received the news that his eldest son, Thembi, had died in a car crash; again he was not allowed to attend the funeral.

COMRADES

Through his long years in prison, Mandela would be sustained by his fellow defendants from the Rivonia Trial, including Walter Sisulu, Indian communist Ahmed Kathrada, Govan Mbeki (father of Thabo Mbeki, later Mandela's successor as South Africa's President), and four others. "The authorities' greatest mistake," Mandela wrote in his autobiography, "was keeping us together, for together our determination was reinforced. Whatever we learned we shared, and by sharing we multiplied whatever courage we had individually. The stronger ones raised up the weaker ones, and both became stronger in the process."

Although speaking was forbidden except during certain brief interludes in the day, the men managed to find ways to communicate and support one another. Veteran political activists to a man, they did what came naturally: they organized. Soon they were operating an executive committee, the High Organ, that served as an A.N.C. leadership-in-exile group, which laid out the prisoners' agenda and maintained internal discipline. Mandela was its chief.

Early in 1965, within a year of their arrival on Robben Island, the prisoners' labor routine changed; they were put to work in a limestone quarry on the island, which was freezing in winter, an oven in summer. Despite their protests, the men were not issued sunglasses for the first three years, and Mandela's eyesight was permanently damaged by the sun's glare. Decades later, a New York *Times* reporter observing Mandela during his first year as South Africa's President caught him wiping his eyes. The former prisoner explained that his tear ducts had been permanently sealed by lime dust and had only been re-opened during an eye operation. He once had been unable to cry, Mandela explained; now he couldn't stop.

The quarry offered a significant advantage over the work of breaking rock in the prison courtyard: here the prisoners were allowed to speak with each other, and the workplace soon became a hothouse for debates on political theory, economic philosophy, South Africa's history and tribal rivalries. It is a powerful image: poorly clothed political prisoners wielding hammers and shovels, digging for limestone while discussing the U.S. Constitution, Karl Marx, Mao Zedong and Gamal Abdel Nassar. The quarry became an al fresco forum for peripatetic philosophers that might have seemed familiar to Socrates. Soon young dissidents sentenced to Robben Island would boast that they were bound for "Mandela University."

The Rivonia Trial prisoners, once isolated from other inmates on the island, now mingled and debated with other political prisoners, including members of Robert Sobukwe's Pan-Africanist Congress, bitter rivals of the A.N.C. in the late 1960s. Later, after the rise of the Black Consciousness movement of the late 1970s, a new group of radical young blacks came to the island; initially they viewed the A.N.C. inmates as out-of-date moderates, but they soon came to admire them and learn from them. The prisoners who followed a fervent communist line and viewed South Africa's woes mainly in class terms fiercely debated those who saw the struggle against racism and apartheid as paramount. Mandela served as leader of the latter group.

Mandela and most of the other A.N.C. prisoners devoted themselves to as much study and learning as they could; the prisoners even taught one another in informal classes at the quarry. Eventually, Mandela was allowed to begin studying for an L.L.B. degree in a correspondence course offered by London University.

After a change in the prison hierarchy in 1971, conditions loosened considerably on the island. Mandela spent hours working in a small garden the prisoners were allowed to cultivate, and inmates were permitted to play sports and even perform plays: Mandela is said to have cut a commanding figure in the role of King Creon in a production of Sophocles' *Antigone*. One prisoner owned a copy of Shakespeare's works, and the precious volume was passed around from hand to hand. In 1977 a few of them signed their favorite passages in the book. Mandela chose these lines from *Julius Caesar*:

> Cowards die many times before their deaths;
> The valiant never taste of death but once.

THE LARGER VIEW

Mandela resolved to treat the small world of Robben Island as a microcosm of South Africa as a whole. Long a believer that every race must have a place in a reborn nation, he worked hard to get to know his mostly Afrikaner guards. Already a student of the language, he increased his studies of the Afrikaner people's history and culture and came to view the warders as fellow victims of apartheid; after all, they had been steeped in racial animosity since infancy. He and the other A.N.C. leaders made a conscious decision not to harbor bitterness or a desire for personal revenge against their captors; they believed the only possibility for a future reconciliation between the races in South Africa would come through working with their oppressors rather than demonizing them.

In 1975 Sisulu and Kathrada encouraged Mandela to begin writing his memoirs, with the notion that they might be published on his 6oth birthday, in 1978. Mandela agreed and produced a lengthy book in only four months. The pages were hidden, buried in a plastic container in the prison courtyard, but they were eventually discovered when a work detail of prisoners accidentally unearthed them. The prison authorities retaliated against this violation of rules by denying Mandela the right to pursue his LL.B. degree at London University for four years. Fortunately, the pages had been copied by inmate Mac Maharaj, who smuggled them out of jail at the end of his sentence in 1976. The memoirs were not published until the 1990s, when they served as the basis for the first two-thirds of the autobiography Mandela completed after his release from prison, *Long Walk to Freedom*.

The strongest challenge to Mandela's peace of mind during these long years was his isolation from his wife and growing children; like many political leaders who forsake family life for a larger purpose, he deeply regretted that he had been forced to choose between his kin and his cause. He fumed at being unable to assist Winnie during her seven-year banishment to Brandfort, a small town in the Free State Province, where she lived as an outsider. Understandably, he put Winnie on a pedestal, making their eventual estrangement all the more painful. His letters to her are filled with expressions of both love and physical longing; his fellow inmates teased the former ladies' man about a *National Geographic* picture he kept in his cell of a nude African woman romping on a beach. He learned with sorrow of the failure of his daughter Maki's marriage in 1978, but could only offer consolation and encouragement in the form of letters. In 1978, when he celebrated his 6oth birthday after serving 14 years of his life term, the occasion was noted in editorials around the world, but authorities handed the prisoner only six cards from family and friends.

LEADER-IN-WAITING

Mandela's days on Robben Island came to an end in April 1982, when he, Sisulu and two other A.N.C. leaders were abruptly taken to Pollsmoor Prison, a modern facility in a Cape Town suburb. The reason for the change of venue was apparently that the white regime believed the A.N.C. leaders were exerting too much influence on the younger opponents of apartheid who had joined them at Robben Island; the doors of "Mandela University" must be firmly closed.

If Robben Island was South Africa's Alcatraz, a private preserve, Pollsmoor was a factory of incarceration, a massive concrete structure with damp cells and little connection to nature. But Mandela was allowed to create a rooftop garden, and he lavished attention on his miniature Eden, spending hours each day tending his plants. The restrictions on his contacts with the outside world were relaxed; he could now send or receive a letter a week, and he received visitors much more often. For the first time he was allowed to watch television, read magazines and keep abreast of world events.

Mandela's visitors often expressed astonishment upon meeting him. Since it was illegal to publish his picture in South Africa, few had any idea what the aging prisoner looked like. Visitors encountered a man who seemed two decades younger than his age, although his face was now deeply lined and his hair gray. Mandela carried himself with authority and spoke with penetrating insight and clarity on South Africa's condition. Condemning the regime's errors, seemingly without bitterness, and insisting that every South African must participate in the birth of a new nation, he struck observers as preparing himself to someday lead his fractured country. "He exuded authority," reported a seven-person team representing the British Commonwealth that met him in 1986, "and received the respect of all around him, including his jailers."

Among those who agreed with that assessment, surprisingly, were officials of the very regime that was keeping him locked up. A 1981 analysis of Mandela's condition by government psychologists reported, "There exists no doubt that Mandela commands all the qualities to be the Number One black leader in South Africa." Yet it would not be until nine years after that report was filed that the government would realize that Mandela was needed to liberate not just his own people but also South Africans of every race and color from the shackles of apartheid.

A Life in Prison

Robben Island is the most famed of Nelson Mandela's prisons, but he occupied three different jails from 1964 to 1990. The following are among the more significant events of his 27 years in captivity.

June 1964
Arrives at Robben Island to begin his life term at age 46

1975
Begins writing memoirs

June 1978
60th birthday

April 1982
Taken from Robben Island to Pollsmoor Prison, where he serves out his term

February 1985
Refuses white regime's offer of freedom in return for renouncing A.N.C. violence

1988
70th birthday marked by world-wide calls for his release

December 1988
Moved to Victor Verster Prison, where he is housed in a private bungalow

July 1989
Begins negotiating with the white regime on terms under which he will be released

Jail *Robben Island, top, is two miles long and eight miles from the mainland. Mandela's cell was spartan but sunny*

Allies and Adversaries

■■■■■

N o man is an island—not even a man imprisoned on one for years. In his long journey to bring justice to South Africa, Nelson Mandela received essential support from a cluster of strong figures, in particular his two closest colleagues, Walter Sisulu and Oliver Tambo. And he was challenged by a host of tough, committed opponents—not only the white politicians of South Africa who supported apartheid but also fellow blacks who questioned his leadership, his strategies and his vision of the nation's future.

Walter Sisulu: 1912-2003

Mandela's mentor met his protégé in 1940, not long after Mandela fled an arranged marriage and holed up in Soweto. Local businessman Sisulu later recalled knowing, "the moment I met him, that this is the man I need" to lead the struggle against apartheid. He urged Mandela to study law and later helped him open South Africa's first black law firm with Oliver Tambo. Sisulu helped found the A.N.C. Youth League in 1943 and led strikes and protests in the 1950s. Convicted in the Rivonia Trial, Sisulu was sentenced to life in prison and was released in 1989, a few months before Mandela. Beloved by those who only respected Mandela, Sisulu shared his friend's uncanny absence of resentment. "Bitterness does not do your cause any good," he said. Above, he stands firm with Mandela in 1990.

Robert Sobukwe: 1924-1978

If Mandela is often likened to Martin Luther King Jr., then Sobukwe was South Africa's Malcolm X. The founder of the Pan Africanist Congress (P.A.C.) broke with the A.N.C. in 1959, embraced the black-power movement that was sweeping across Africa and declared that whites and even mixed-race coloureds had no place in the antiapartheid cause. His harsher line also embraced violence against the government.

Born in the town of Graaff Reinet, Sobukwe was raised in poverty (unlike Mandela), and he was also a more dazzling orator than the older man. Arrested in 1960, Sobukwe—called "the Professor" by admiring associates—was imprisoned in a Pretoria jail for a time with Mandela. They came to respect each other, but never reconciled their divergent approaches to the struggle against apartheid. Sobukwe later spent years in solitary confinement, an ordeal from which he never fully recovered. He died of lung cancer in 1978.

H.F. Verwoerd: 1901-1966

"These people are criminals, communist criminals, just as any spy caught and executed in the United States," South Africa's Prime Minister from 1958 to 1966 declared to his Parliament about Mandela and the other defendants at the Rivonia trial. The German-educated Verwoerd was one of the chief architects of apartheid—a key figure in formalizing South Africa's tradition and culture of racial oppression into law and policy. Among his designs: the plan to create 10 Bantustans, or black homelands, thereby leaving the remaining 87% of the country's land area to whites. Verwoerd was stabbed to death in 1966 by a mentally unbalanced government clerk from a mixed-race family.

Oliver Tambo: 1917-1993

Expelled with Mandela from Fort Hare University in 1940 for political activism, Tambo and his friend later became law partners. They were a study in contrasts: Mandela energetic and given to high-flown rhetoric, Tambo quiet and scholarly. When other A.N.C. leaders were imprisoned in the early 1960s, Tambo fled South Africa and led the banned group from exile for the next 30 years, showing a steely, ruthless resolve. After claiming responsibility for a 1983 Pretoria bomb blast that killed 18 people, Tambo told TIME, "We have offered the other cheek so many times that there is no cheek left to turn." As Mandela emerged from the shadows, Tambo retreated into them: in 1989 he suffered a stroke that removed him from the stage only months before Mandela's triumphant release.

Desmond Tutu: 1931-

The ebullient Anglican archbishop and 1984 winner of the Nobel Peace Prize wields enormous moral authority in South Africa; with Mandela, he embodied the dreams of the people. A rare figure who commanded the respect of both blacks and whites, for decades he performed a political high-wire act, counseling both resistance and restraint.

In 1985 Tutu faced down an angry mob of blacks, who were determined to burn alive a black man suspected of being a police informant. When Tutu threatened to "pack up and leave this beautiful country that I love so passionately and so deeply" if they did so, the crowd dispersed. In the 1980s, government security officials often heeded his calls to release prisoners and withdraw patrols in exchange for pledges of peace; they knew Tutu could deliver. In 1986 he bravely admonished a stadium full of protesters, "I know we all want freedom, but we must get it in a disciplined manner." Again, the crowd went home without bloodshed.

The cleric could also summon words of anger: when U.S. President Ronald Reagan delivered a disappointing speech on sanctions, Tutu scowled that "the West, for my part, can go to hell." Mandela called upon Tutu to lead the Truth and Reconciliation Commission in 1995, which offered extremists on both sides amnesty for acts of political violence in exchange for a full confession. But Tutu's personal high point may have come a year earlier, when he voted for the first time. "I am about two inches taller than before I arrived," the diminutive prelate joked after filling out his ballot.

Joe Slovo: 1926-1995

An early leader of the A.N.C. guerrilla wing, M.K., longtime communist Slovo became the first white member of the A.N.C.'s executive council in 1985 and chief of the South African Communist Party in 1987. Wanted by South Africa's security forces, Slovo spent decades in exile and paid a high price for his commitment: in 1982 his wife was killed by a mail bomb. Pardoned in 1990, he became a key negotiator in the talks that ended apartheid, then served as a minister in Mandela's government.

Thabo Mbeki: 1942-

The British-educated Mbeki is the son of Mandela's old A.N.C. colleague and fellow Robben Island prisoner, Govan Mbeki. He spent 28 years in exile as a diplomat and fund raiser for the A.N.C. Succeeding Mandela in 1999 as South Africa's second black President, Mbeki steered his nation through a series of crises, angering Mandela by discounting the threat posed to South Africans by HIV/AIDS. He was re-elected to a second five-year term in 2004, but disputes with his controversial A.N.C. colleague Jacob Zuma, rising crime rates, nationwide power shortages and his refusal to condemn Robert Mugabe's reign of terror in neighboring Zimbabwe led his own party to withdraw its support, and he resigned in September 2008, a year before his term ended.

F.W. de Klerk: 1936-

As the cold war ended, the canny scion of a political dynasty who wanted to be South Africa's leader saw the writing on the wall. Frederik Willem de Klerk allied himself with the "enlightened" wing of the National Party, which argued that, as communism unraveled, the West no longer had any reason to support a regime that was increasingly viewed as a political and moral disaster.

In February 1989, following President P.W. Botha's stroke, De Klerk was chosen head of the National Party, and in September of that year he became President of South Africa. Within six months, he lifted the ban on the A.N.C.and other black groups and began releasing political prisoners,culminating with Mandela. In 1992 De Klerk presided over a whites-only referendum in which voters were asked to approve his radical transformation of the nation; they endorsed his policies by a resounding majority of 68%. Two years later, De Klerk became Deputy President in the administration of the man he had freed from prison. He retired from public life in 1997.

P.W. Botha: 1916-2006

Known as "the Great Crocodile" for his blustery temper, South Africa's Prime Minister from 1978 to 1984 and President from 1984 to 1989 was an unapologetic advocate for apartheid. "We shall not be forced to sell out our proud heritage," Pieter Willem Botha defiantly told the world in a 1989 speech, referring to international pressure for reform. Attempts at piecemeal concessions seemed only to stiffen the resolve of Botha's adversaries: his 1985 offer to free Mandela if he would forswear political violence brought the famous rebuke that "only free men can negotiate; prisoners cannot enter into contracts."

Botha's heels (and those of the government he led) remained firmly dug in, until a major stroke forced him into retirement in 1989. Mandela once stated that he preferred the outright racial bigotry of Botha to what he perceived as the more subtle racism of the man with whom he negotiated the end to apartheid, Botha's successor, F.W. de Klerk.

Margaret Thatcher: 1925-2013

"A typical terrorist organization," the British Prime Minister labeled the A.N.C. in a 1987 speech, adding that anyone who thought Nelson Mandela would ever govern South Africa was "living in cloud cuckoo land." Shunning "utterly repugnant" economic sanctions against South Africa, Thatcher and her ally, U.S. President Ronald Reagan, viewed that nation through the prism of the cold war and saw the white regime as a bulwark against communism. The "Iron Lady" went on to gamble British prestige in the region on Zulu chief Buthelezi, backing him as an alternative to Mandela. In July 1996 President Mandela addressed both houses of Britain's Parliament and was cheered; he refused to meet with Thatcher, by then a backbencher.

Mangosuthu Buthelezi: 1928-

After Mandela's release from prison, the single greatest threat to his vision for a united, multiracial South Africa came not from the nation's whites, but from Zulu chief Buthelezi, founder of the 1.5 million-member Inkatha Freedom Party. An avowed capitalist, Buthelezi was bitterly critical of the A.N.C.'s left-leaning orientation; he condemned economic sanctions and collaborated with government security forces. As the first free elections in the nation's history drew near in 1994, he threatened to boycott them. A week before the election, Buthelezi backed down; he later joined Mandela's government.

Free Mandela!

◼▬

WHEN NELSON MANDELA AND THE OTHER DEFENDANTS AT THE Rivonia Trial were carted off to jail in 1964, in theory never to be heard from again, the apartheid government and its white supporters breathed a quiet sigh of relief. They shared a widespread sense that the book had finally been closed on the leaders of the opposition to South Africa's racial policies—and perhaps even a feeling of smug self-congratulation at the clever restraint with which the regime had decided not to execute the defendants, thus depriving the African National Congress of ready-made martyrs for their cause.

The A.N.C. had other plans, and a martyr in waiting: in the years that followed, Nelson Mandela would become one of the most famous people in the world, his aura of mystery and power all the more enhanced by his invisibility. In the vacuum of information, Mandela became a blank screen onto which all sorts of dreams, hopes and superhuman powers could be projected. When he was first sentenced to prison, the wider world scarcely paused to take notice. Two decades later, his name seemed to be everywhere: it was on the banners of demonstrators from Pretoria to New York City to Paris; it was cheered on college campuses around the globe; it was damned and praised in congresses and parliaments; it even rang on the lips of British schoolkids who sang along to the infectious, bubbling beat of *Free Nelson Mandela,* the 1984 hit single recorded in the U.K. by the Special AKA and produced by Elvis Costello.

How was a regional rebel transformed into a global icon of conscience? The canonization of a phantom was largely due to the simple justice of his cause and the increasingly apparent horrors of apartheid, but it was also the result of a shrewdly managed campaign by the A.N.C. to make Mandela the global symbol of opposition to South Africa's racist regime.

The process took time: Mandela's imprisonment decapitated the militant Spear of the Nation (M.K.) wing of the party, effectively shutting down the activities of the guerrillas for years. And with many of its key leaders imprisoned with Mandela on Robben Island, the A.N.C.

Rock star *When Mandela was sentenced to a life term in prison in 1964, his name and cause were little known outside his home country, although that year a student at Britain's Cambridge University wrote a simple two-word plea that would later resound around the world—including at Mandela's 70th birthday party rock concert in London, bottom photo, in 1988*

On the march *In 1986 demonstrators in Paris joined the worldwide protests that denounced Mandela's imprisonment, as the South African regime's apartheid policies seemed increasingly at odds with the liberating tides of 20th century history*

battled simply to keep itself alive; the activist group's head, Oliver Tambo, fled South Africa and set up operations in exile, communicating at first only occasionally with his imprisoned colleagues. In the late 1960s a fresh wave of black rebels captured the imagination of South Africa's restive township youths, and by 1976, when the Soweto riots exposed the injustices of apartheid for all the world to see, it seemed that the charismatic Stephen Biko would lead apartheid's foes. That threat to the regime was soon removed, and this time around there was no trial or prisoner to generate publicity: Biko died mysteriously in police custody, case closed.

By the end of the 1970s, the A.N.C. had reached a low point, seemingly shunted aside, as the antiapartheid movement grappled for a leader and a fresh focus. Yet in this dark period, the first shoots of renewal were beginning to appear. Less than a year after the Soweto riots, the United Nations imposed an arms embargo on the country. It was a gentle rebuke, to be sure—the measure was used to head off one calling for economic sanctions that would have been more effective—but the measure signaled the opening notes in a chorus of worldwide condemnation and isolation of South Africa that would swell with each passing year.

In 1980 Tambo and other A.N.C. leaders in exile launched a campaign to make Mandela's incarceration the foremost symbol of opposition to apartheid. That March the Johannesburg *Sunday Post* signed on to the program, under the headline FREE MANDELA. The simple exhortation—short enough to fit on a bumper sticker or button and graffiti-friendly—caught on. South Africa's antiapartheid whites embraced it; a resolution endorsed by the U.N. Security Council echoed it. It was proclaimed from pulpits, chanted by children, spun into song. A film about Biko's life, *Cry Freedom,* put the plight of black South Africans on the screen, while Mbongeni Ngema's *Sarafina!* and the dramas of Athol Fugard moved theater audiences around the world, and the blistering antiapartheid novels of Nadine Gordimer and Alan Paton, some of them decades old, attracted a new, wider audience of readers around the world.

COLD WAR CHILLS

Pretoria still had cards to play, however, against this outpouring of support for Mandela and the A.N.C., in particular the ongoing struggle between communism and capitalism. The A.N.C.'s much publicized alliance with the South African Communist Party was a critical tool for the white government; for decades the authorities worked to establish the linkage between opposition to apartheid and support for communism, christening legal measures designed to harass the A.N.C. with names like the Suppression of Communism Act. Mandela, the government constantly assured its detractors, was nothing more than a communist terrorist. During the cold war, the U.S. embraced all manner of tyrannous regimes abroad, provided they joined the anticommunist cause. South Africa deftly positioned itself within this camp.

For no nation was the relationship with South Africa more complicated or more troubling than for Britain. The British enjoyed commercial and political ties to South Africa that were centuries old and shared its government's opposition to communism. South Africa's government leveraged both the commercial and political relationships to give capitalist governments around the world a stake in its survival. "Each trade agreement, each bank loan, each new investment is another brick in the wall of our continued existence," declared South Africa's Prime Minister John Vorster in 1972. By the mid-1980s, nearly half of all foreign money invested in South Africa came from Britain, and almost 10% of all British capital invested abroad went there. If independent politically, South Africa was economically a British colony.

As nation after nation announced economic sanctions and arms embargoes against South Africa, Britain and the U.S. remained intransigent. Under conservative leaders Ronald Reagan and Margaret Thatcher, both nations adopted a policy of quiet persuasion—"constructive engagement" was the diplomatic term—rather than more potent sanctions. But that strategy increasingly came to seem an excuse for foot dragging while South Africa was burning. In 1986 even many Republicans in the U.S. Senate joined with Democrats to override the popular Reagan's veto of a bill establishing tough sanctions against South Africa. The final vote: 78 to 21.

BANKS BALK

Disgust with apartheid also led to wider calls for corporate divestiture, which proved even more devastating than sanctions to the South Africans. As a rule, sanctions prohibited only the sending of new capital to the nation. Divestiture required corporations to sell off existing businesses in South Africa as well as shares in the nation's firms. By late 1986, more than 70 large U.S. companies had embraced divestiture. As major international banks began withdrawing credit from tumultuous South Africa, it became clear that the government's moral bankruptcy was driving it to financial bankruptcy.

Nelson Mandela's 70th birthday in 1988 was celebrated with a chorus of cries for his release that girdled the globe. In London, 72,000 people attended a birthday rock concert at Wembley Stadium; 200 million more viewers tuned in on TV. A two-word plea now united college students in Oxford and Paris, clerics in Detroit and Dublin, intellectuals in Bangalore and impoverished blacks in South Africa's township shebeens: Free Mandela!

Igniting hatred *The vehicle of a suspected police informer, set afire by suspicious fellow blacks, burned at the funeral of four victims of a hand-grenade assault at Duduza, in 1985*

SELWYN TAIT—TIME LIFE PICTURES—GETTY IMAGES

A Nation
In Flames

T HE IMPRISONMENT OF NELSON MAN-
dela and most of the other leaders of the
African National Congress in 1964 dealt
a serious blow to the antiapartheid cause.
Yet the system's injustices were a recipe for
resentment, breeding 10 new opponents
for every one that was jailed. Despite the regime's temporary success, a fuse had been lighted; it now began burning
slowly but inexorably toward a powder keg of racial hatred.
When it exploded, as Mandela and the A.N.C. had long
predicted it would, it plunged the entire nation into a cata-
clysm of blood, violence and revenge.

The first steps in South Africa's march toward self-immo-
lation took place almost imperceptibly, as a nation that had
aspired to be a European-style parliamentary democracy
(at least for the white minority that was legally entitled to
vote) increasingly took on the trappings of a police state.
In the decade after the Rivonia Trial, ad hoc measures
instituted during various temporary states of emergency
became permanent. Laws like the Internal Security Act, the
Terrorism Act, and the Suppression of Communism Act
empowered the police to arrest anyone without a warrant,

then hold and interrogate that person for weeks at a time, without filing charges. In more serious cases, the police could keep even the fact of the arrest secret, deny the suspect access to a lawyer and hold the detainee indefinitely, bypassing the formal justice system.

Even as police power was legally expanded, a grim array of extralegal tools was placed in the hands of security agents. In the mid-1960s South African police began arresting anti-apartheid leaders, only to have them "commit suicide"—or tumble down a flight of stairs or fall out of a chair and suffer a broken neck—while in custody, always under mysterious circumstances that were never investigated. When family or friends of the deceased tried to investigate, they would often be arrested themselves, along with their lawyers and medical experts. In one 1969 case, an official government report responding to an inquiry after a death acknowledges only "an unnamed person who died in an undisclosed place on an undisclosed date." Dozens of South African deaths were officially reported the same way.

Those the police couldn't arrest (or didn't wish to be observed taking into custody) often perished when letter bombs exploded in their faces or when assassins who were waiting in ambush fired a well-aimed bullet into their body. The first method claimed the life of Ruth Frist, the wife of the A.N.C.'s most senior white leader, the guerrilla chief and communist supporter Joe Slovo, in 1982. The latter method killed anthropologist David Webster, also white, who was researching an academic paper on the mysterious deaths of apartheid opponents; he was gunned down outside his Johannesburg home in 1989 by three white men in a car. Years after the fact, government security agents would confess to the bombing of the London office of the A.N.C. in 1982 and the assassination of a number of A.N.C. leaders while they were living in exile elsewhere in Africa, especially in Angola and Mozambique.

A HERO CUT DOWN

The single most brazen act of murderous violence committed by South Africa's police was directed against a black rival of the A.N.C. who came to prominence in the late 1960s, Stephen Biko. The brutal murder of this charismatic leader, which police tried to cover up as yet another "accident," electrified black South Africans and once again put the nation's apartheid police state in the headlines around the world.

Biko emerged as a galvanizing figure at a time when the A.N.C. and the virulently anti-white Pan-Africanist Congress had been mired in a years-long slump. By the mid-1970s the banning of both organizations, combined with brutally effective police repression, had lowered their profiles and drastically curtailed their activities. Although exiled A.N.C. chief Oliver Tambo was raising a guerrilla army and training it in nearby African nations, his hopes of waging a sustained war against the regime were far from being realized.

Biko—whose motto was "Black man, you are on your own"—filled this vacuum with a movement, Black Consciousness, that offered immediate psychological liberation while it promised political and economic freedoms in the long term. The movement's ideal catalyst was supplied, unintentionally, by the white government. In 1974 Pretoria decreed that all black students must learn Afrikaans, the Dutch dialect that was apartheid's mother tongue and thus detested by blacks: Archbishop Desmond Tutu called it "the language of the oppressor."

Resentment of Afrikaans was festering on the last day of April 1976, when pupils at the Orlando West Junior School in Soweto went on strike, refusing to attend classes. Within days their protest spread to other black schools in Soweto and then across South Africa.

Murder *A victim of necklacing is incinerated in the Transkei in 1985. The grisly method of execution was introduced to South Africa in the 1980s; Winnie Mandela was excoriated after she appeared to endorse the practice in a speech*

Grief *The poster at right features a picture that moved the world: friend Mbuyisa Makubu carries the body of Hector Peterson, 13, the first victim of police violence in the Soweto riots of June 1976. Sam Nzima's photograph was widely reproduced, but apartheid-era restrictions kept him from realizing the profit he deserved from licensing its use*

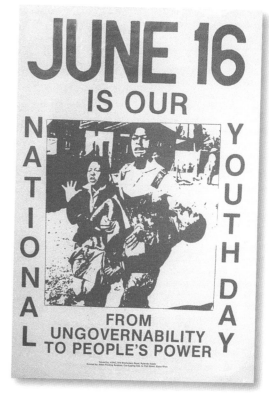

JUNE 16 IS OUR NATIONAL YOUTH DAY

FROM UNGOVERNABILITY TO PEOPLE'S POWER

Biko, 1977

Biko: Apartheid's Martyr

A former medical student who was handsome, brilliant, eloquent and charismatic, Stephen Biko might have become another Nelson Mandela—if South Africa's white regime had allowed him to. Biko, like Mandela a Xhosa, formed the all-black South African Students' Organization (S.A.S.O.) in 1969. With Robert Sobukwe of the Pan-Africanist Congress, Biko advocated "Black Consciousness," a form of African nationalism that emphasized self-reliance, pride in Africa's cultural and tribal heritage and the throwing off of "the shackles of servitude." The term "blacks," once avoided by natives as racist, was now embraced by Biko and a new generation of rebels determined to celebrate their heritage.

Heavily influenced by the black power movement in the U.S. as well as the revolutionary theories popular in the 1960s, Biko preached that "the most potent weapon in the hands of the oppressor is the mind of the oppressed." The S.A.S.O. movement swept across South Africa in the early 1970s, until alarmed authorities banned Biko and seven other leaders—just as they had banned Mandela and the A.N.C. almost two decades earlier.

Biko became the regime's most hated foe when he led the demonstrations that erupted in the Soweto riots in 1976. A year later, he suffered a severe head wound while in police custody in Port Elizabeth in the Eastern Cape province. Still breathing after his assault, Biko was tossed into the back of a police van and chained naked to the floor for the 700-mile drive to Pretoria, much of it over unpaved roads. Biko died just after the vehicle reached the capital. His white interrogators described his injuries as the result of "a scuffle" that was aggravated by a hunger strike and, later, as a failed suicide attempt. In 1997 five white South African policemen admitted to murdering Biko; the Truth and Reconciliation Commission chose not to try them.

Stephen Biko penned his own epitaph, once writing, "It is better to die for an idea that will live, than to live for an idea that will die."

Biko and other protest leaders called a massive opposition rally for June 16. The protest in Soweto began as a peaceful march, but it began to spiral out of control when policemen used tear gas in a ham-fisted attempt to disperse the crowd. Some of the gagging students surged forward, which prompted one police officer to fire a single shot into the air. The sound of gunfire panicked everyone. Police began firing wildly into the crowd, and protesters broke into a full-scale riot. Among the first to die was Hector Peterson, 13. The photograph of the young victim's body being carried from the scene quickly traveled around the world, becoming an iconic image of the price of apartheid. Three more Soweto children were gunned down by police on June 16, along with 20 adults. Before the day's ordeal was over, more than 600 people were dead around the nation.

DESCENT INTO ANARCHY

The reverberations of the Soweto riots echoed through South Africa in ways large and small for years to come. One immediate result: the police made a target of the protest's most visible leader, Biko. His death in September 1977 stunned a nation that had seemed inured to violence and galvanized the black community's opposition to apartheid. More than 15,000 people attended the martyr's funeral.

The Soweto massacre also revitalized the A.N.C., providing the organization with a new mandate for revolutionary change and a vast new reservoir of black anger to tap. Mandela would later recall the early-1970s torpor as the darkest period for the A.N.C., a time when it came dangerously close to being irrelevant. Yet only a few years after the Soweto riots, a poll taken by the Johannesburg *Star* found that nearly as many South African blacks endorsed the A.N.C. as all other anti-apartheid groups combined.

With Biko removed from the scene, moral leadership once again was placed on Mandela's shoulders, despite his imprisonment. He won new admirers after the Soweto incidents when members of the new generation of hot-headed antiapartheid leaders were imprisoned with him and came under his influence—it was around this time that the Robben Island prison came to be called "Mandela University." Ironically, prison was perhaps the only place where Mandela was safe during these years. The government of South Africa was, in the eyes of the world, directly responsible for the personal security of its most conspicuous detainee. Biko's death ensured Mandela could not be dispatched without provoking a civil war.

In the 1980s, as the struggle against apartheid intensified, increasing factionalism among the system's foes bred a rise in black-on-black violence. In black homelands and townships, where high unemployment and poor education were toxic breeding grounds for unrest and crime, militant youths began punishing factional foes by "necklacing" them—placing a gasoline-filled tire around their upper bodies, then igniting the tire.

The factional flames were fanned by government security agents, it would be proved years later, who used moles and informers to nurture suspicion among black leaders, start false rumors of police cooperation and even supply arms to the factions. The regime was having it both ways: it was funding black-on-black violence, then exploiting the horrors that resulted as justification for the police state and proof to a watching world that South Africa's blacks were incapable of governing themselves. In another circle of violence, police often fired into crowds at demonstrations. When protesters were killed, their funerals would breed new demonstrations, at which the police often ended up firing into the crowds once again.

Front lines *At top, white students protesting apartheid policies in Cape Town in 1985 took shelter from police gas behind posters of their hero, Mandela. The images themselves were illegal: from 1964 until 1988, it was against the law to print photographs of Mandela in South Africa. In the bottom picture, police officers wield sjamboks with a will in 1985 as they break up a protest march heading for Pollsmoor Prison, where Mandela was detained from 1982 until late 1988*

RACE WARS

In the early 1980s antiapartheid strife began to spread to white sections of South Africa. Roused from its mid-1970s slumber, the A.N.C.'s Umkhonto we Sizwe (M.K.) arm finally put together a viable guerrilla army. Based in the so-called Front Line States of nations situated close to South Africa and sympathetic to the A.N.C.—Angola, Botswana, Lesotho, Mozambique, Tanzania, Zambia and Zimbabwe—the group of 6,000 fighters, armed with weapons provided by the A.N.C.'s allies in the communist bloc, regularly staged cross-border raids and bombing attacks. As when Mandela had run the M.K., those acts of sabotage were initially designed to cause maximum chaos but minimal loss of life. More than 80 attacks in the early 1980s caused millions of dollars in damage but led to only eight deaths.

By 1983, however, mounting frustration with the slow pace of change led to a dramatic escalation of A.N.C. activity. In May of that year, a car bomb placed by M.K. agents exploded on a crowded sidewalk in Pretoria, killing 18 people. The South African government responded by sending its air force to bomb A.N.C. camps in Mozambique and began funneling arms and money to antigovernment guerrilla troops in many of the Front Line States, triggering regional wars that lasted another decade.

In the black townships, the situation continued to deteriorate. As a TIME cover story reported in 1985, "Every white South African city and town, even the smallest dorp (village), has its Soweto, its satellite township where the blacks live. It is where the paved road ends and the dirt begins. Asphalt highways cut through Soweto, but the side streets disappear quickly into dust or mud. The smaller the township, the fewer the amenities. Some communities have only a few electric lights, and none in individual homes. Some have only one outside privy for a row of houses. Night soil is collected by a clanking tractor and trailer ... political ferment is accentuated by slum living, lack of amenities, overcrowding, crime and the breakdown of family life. The despair of township life, the prospect of no breakout from such confinement, is felt most keenly by the young."

The situation was unsustainable. As tension mounted, Prime Minister P.W. Botha tried to satisfy apartheid's foes with half a loaf: he offered to release Mandela from prison if he and the A.N.C. would forswear the use of violence. Mandela's reply to the government (and to his fellow black South Africans) was read aloud by his daughter Zinzi at an A.N.C. rally on Feb. 10, 1985. It was the first time Africans had heard Mandela's voice (albeit by proxy) in more than two decades, and he rose to the occasion with words that will ring down through the ages: "Only free men can negotiate. Prisoners cannot enter into contracts ... I will not give any undertaking at a time when I and you, the people, are not free. Your freedom and mine cannot be separated. I will return."

ENDGAME

On July 20, 1985, South Africans tuned in to the 6 o'clock news to see live coverage of a screaming black crowd at a funeral in the township of Duduza, outside Johannesburg. Apparently acting on the accusation of one pointed finger and one shout of "Informer!," the mob turned on a young black woman, who was quickly stoned, beaten, stripped and burned to death, all on nationwide television. At 8 p.m., saying that "this state of affairs can no longer be tolerated," Prime Minister P.W. Botha announced that emergency regulations would go into effect in major black regions of the nation. Once again, turning the screws only served to aggravate the situation; Botha was forced to renew the state of emergency every year for four years. During this ghastly period, the A.N.C. launched a new campaign designed to demonstrate it could render South Africa "ungovernable." As riots erupted with ever greater frequency, it was clear that the nation was on a suicide course. The A.N.C. campaign succeeded in proving its point: the National Party could no longer govern South Africa. Only a dramatic break from the failed policies of the past, it seemed, could avert the armageddon of a racial bloodbath.

As more parliaments in other nations enacted sanctions, as more international banks withdrew credit lines, as communist regimes wobbled in Eastern Europe and the Kremlin's global influence faded, as more white South Africans demanded to know why they were shunned when they traveled abroad and their nation's athletes were banned from the Olympic Games, even Botha began to recognize the inevitable. One day in 1989 he received a most unlikely visitor at his residence for a chat: Nelson Mandela. Four decades after the iron bars of legal apartheid descended upon South Africa, and 25 years after the jail doors closed upon the "Black Pimpernel," the doors were finally ready to swing open—for the nation as a whole and for the man who had promised his people he would return.

Uprising *TIME* put the anti-apartheid protests on its Aug. 5, 1985, cover

Mandela: Closer to Freedom

Through much of the 1980s, as South Africa burned, Nelson Mandela and the government engaged in a protracted courtship dance. The worldwide "Free Mandela" campaign shone a bright new spotlight on the prisoner, who came into more frequent contact with key government figures after he was moved to Pollsmoor Prison in 1982. Impressed with his intelligence and commanding presence, they began to see him as the one figure who might be able to bring the nation's restless blacks under control.

Such hopes faded after Mandela ringingly refused Prime Minister P.W. Botha's 1985 offer to set him free in exchange for the A.N.C.'s promise to renounce violence. So white leaders were surprised a year later when Mandela, acting without consulting his A.N.C. colleagues, wrote a letter to Minister of Justice Kobie Coetsee, proposing "talks about talks." Coetsee finally arranged to meet secretly with Mandela, beginning the prisoner's journey to freedom.

The two men met 12 times in jail from 1987 to 1990. By 1988 Mandela was meeting regularly with a government team, trying to hammer out a deal for his freedom. Mandela came down with tuberculosis in August 1988. He spent six weeks in a hospital—where he charmed white nurses with his warmth—but he recovered and the talks resumed.

In December 1988 Mandela was secretly moved to Victor Verster Prison, 35 miles outside Cape Town. There he was housed not in a jail cell but in a pleasant bungalow with a garden, swimming pool and cook; white warder Jack Swart became fast friends with his "prisoner." But this gilded cage was still a cage: the flower garden was bugged. In 1989 Mandela was taken to visit P.W. Botha at his official residence: to his surprise, the Prime Minister poured his tea. Guards began driving Mandela around the countryside, preparing him for a return to normal life. He was now able to communicate frequently with exiled A.N.C. chief Oliver Tambo, keeping him abreast of the talks.

The negotiations intensified, surviving a change in leadership after Botha suffered a stroke and was replaced by F.W. de Klerk. The rebel who had arrived at Robben Island as a despised criminal was now an indispensable man who was being groomed to become the savior of his nation. As TIME would put it when Mandela finally walked out of prison, "Mandela is a hero, a man like those described by author Joseph Campbell, who has emerged from a symbolic grave, reborn, made great and filled with creative power."

Freedom!

■ ▬ ▬ ▬

L ATE IN THE AFTERNOON OF SUNDAY, FEB. 11, 1990, THE GATES OF Victor Verster Prison opened, and the historic moment millions of people around the planet had awaited for years was at hand: Nelson Mandela, the world's most noted prisoner of conscience, walked into the sunlight of freedom. The timing of his release was strangely apt, for the hour was getting very late for South Africans to find some—any!—accommodation between its deeply polarized races. And Mandela himself, at 71 years old, could naturally be assumed to be in the twilight of his life as well.

The release of Mandela came at a moment in history when all things seemed possible. Only three months before, the world had watched in wonder as the Berlin Wall, brutal symbol of the cold war that had divided the West and the Soviet bloc since the late 1940s, was torn down, and East and West Germans embraced as brothers. Now one of the globe's last great fortresses of fear—South Africa's hateful system of apartheid—was also cracking wide open, and its foremost opponent would be a free man who would negotiate with his former jailers to form a new, more just nation.

The hopes and dreams of millions of South Africans, black and white alike, rested squarely on the shoulders of this aging Thembu nobleman. In the days and years to come, Mandela would be called upon to play many parts: hero and unifier, healer and savior, politician and idol. Could any one man—let alone one who had been cut off from the flow of daily life for more than 27 years—live up to such great expectations? The burden on Mandela's shoulders was enormous as he walked away from more than 10,000 days in prison and immediately waded into the thick of South African politics.

Unseen legend *With no new pictures of Mandela available, newspapers anticipating his release ran photos from the early 1960s*

Triumph *Reunited after 27 years, Nelson and Winnie Mandela greet cheering throngs outside the prison*

The suspense was unbearable: here was one of the most famous persons in the world, yet only a very few people had cast eyes on him for almost three decades. As the cameras zoomed in on the hero of the hour, they revealed a tall, slim man walking upright, his head held high—and his right arm held high as well, fist clenched in the familiar black-power salute of African nationalism. By his side was his long-suffering, controversial wife Winnie, his partner in opposition to apartheid. The cameras revealed Mandela's bearing to be that of a much younger man—a first clear sign of his triumph over imprisonment.

The scene was confused. Mandela's release had been advanced from its appointed time a few days by authorities in hopes of avoiding chaos, but the strategy backfired, and their hasty preparations for the historic event proved insufficient. Winnie's party, which had flown in from Johannesburg, arrived late, complicating matters. As the couple walked through the prison gates, crowds swamped them; no one seemed to be in charge as a loose scrum of media descended on the couple, hidden at first in the ruckus. Within minutes, Nelson and Winnie were hustled into a waiting car and driven to Cape Town, where Mandela was scheduled to address the nation from the steps of city hall. On the 45-minute drive, Mandela was stunned to see white families standing by the roadside, waiting to hail his motorcade, their fists raised in the black-power salute. It was an early vision of how much his nation had changed in his absence, and he stopped his car to greet and thank one of the families.

Victory Lap *Mandela and Archbishop Desmond Tutu stroll in Johannesburg after the prisoner's release*

AN OPPORTUNITY MISSED

When the motorcade arrived in Cape Town, more confusion reigned; admirers besieged the couple's car, pounding on it ecstatically with their fists. As Mandela recalled in his autobiography, "Inside it sounded like a massive hailstorm ... I felt as though the crowd might very well kill us with their love."

The speech was his first opportunity to leverage the enormous attention generated by his release, but Mandela didn't make the most of his big moment: he had been shoved in front of international cameras before his eyes could even adjust to the glare of a world he had barely seen since 1962. Never a great orator, he now spoke in the plodding manner of a lawyer as he read by-the-book remarks that had been all too obviously vetted by his colleagues in the A.N.C. leadership and their communist allies.

The speech made clear that years of imprisonment had not taken the fight out of Mandela. "Now is the time to intensify the struggle," he exhorted. But some of his words thoroughly alarmed many of his white listeners, who were particularly discomfited by Mandela's appeal for continued Western sanctions, his call for a "fundamental restructuring of our political and economic systems" and his effusive salute to the South African Communist Party. That party's star had fallen everywhere around the world in the previous years—except in South Africa, where the struggle against apartheid had given it focus and purpose—and the tribute to his allies, however deserved, made Mandela seem all too clearly out-of-step with history's arc.

But if his initial speech raised some fears, Mandela soon put matters right. The next day he held his first press conference, charming international reporters with his warmth and humor and expressing for the first time his astonishing lack of bitterness over his long imprisonment. On Feb. 13 he spoke to an overexcited, largely black crowd of 100,000 in a Soweto soccer stadium and adopted a markedly different tone, stressing reconciliation and discipline. "I must make it clear that the level of crime in our townships is unhealthy and must be eliminated as a matter of urgency," he urged his black listeners.

Mandela denounced those blacks who "use violence against our people" and demanded that black students return to the classroom. He sought to heal open wounds in the black community by reaching out to those "who out of ignorance have collaborated with apartheid in the past." And he spoke unyieldingly on the issues that most angered blacks: substandard schools, poor housing, inadequate wages and their continued lack of a vote.

While his rhetoric was forceful, Mandela signaled that he was a magnanimous and reasonable man, reassuring the skittish white community: "We must clearly demonstrate our goodwill to our white compatriots and convince them ... that a South Africa without apartheid will be a better home for all." Here was the first clear indication that Mandela could be the leader his nation needed—one who could reach across all barriers and represent South Africans of every race. Days later, when TIME's Scott MacLeod asked him if his sacrifice had been worth the price, he declared: "Yes, it was worth it. To go to prison because of your convictions, and be prepared to suffer for what you believe in, is something worthwhile. It is an achievement for a man to do his duty on earth irrespective of the consequences."

After the speech, Mandela was finally able to savor the moments he had long imagined during his ordeal in prison. He returned to his home in Soweto and enjoyed a days-long reunion with his extended family, old friends and A.N.C. supporters—even as a huge contingent of the international press surrounded the modest family home.

FORECAST: STORMY

Outside those walls, not all South Africans were rejoicing: ultra-right-wing militants were gearing for battle. The Conservative Party, made up of right-wingers who had broken away from the ruling National Party because they considered it too conciliatory, brought treason charges against Mandela and two other antiapartheid leaders and demanded that they be investigated, while an anti-A.N.C. protest march in Pretoria drew 15,000 whites.

Their cause, however, had been effectively negated by Mandela's commanding dignity and self-confidence. More a myth than a man, he now felt an entire nation's hopes resting on his shoulders. Yet his very presence outside a jail had already changed the political landscape. No longer were questions of South Africa's future hung up on the issue of his release: now all parties could begin the still more difficult task of establishing a new political system.

Mandela promised to be up to the task. As TIME noted the week of his release, "The burden of his legend seems almost more than any one man can bear. A study in dignity, intelligence and unflappability, he is showing amazing grace as he moves from his symbolic role as a political prisoner to the more demanding one of a political activist." The man whose great work had been simply to survive 27 years in prison with his spirit, mind and will intact, now faced an even more difficult challenge: to heal a nation.

Homecoming *Mandela receives a welcoming hug from a relative, above; at right, both whites and blacks celebrate Mandela's release on Feb. 11, 1990. At bottom, in a scene that could not be imagined when Mandela began serving his life term in 1964, students of all races greet the released prisoner*

American Dreamer

■▬▬▬

WHEN NELSON MANDELA WAS RELEASED FROM HIS LONG imprisonment, he dreamed above all of spending time with his family. But that luxury was denied him. The terrible conditions within his nation, which seemed so close to exploding over its racial tensions, demanded that he devote his full attention to the task that South Africa's leaders had now acknowledged by his release that only he could perform: the remaking of the nation.

Mandela and his African National Congress colleagues believed they must immediately capitalize on the worldwide excitement sparked by his release from prison. So during his first few months of freedom, Mandela became a global ambassador for the A.N.C. In March 1990, only weeks after his release, he met world leaders at Namibia's independence celebrations; in April he wowed 70,000 fans at a London rock concert in his honor; in June the 71-year-old set out on a 45-day tour of 13 nations on three continents. His mission: to call for the continuation of sanctions against South Africa's regime, to raise funds for the A.N.C.— and to rally its supporters by bearing witness to the uplifting story of his long incarceration and recent release.

When the news leaked that Mandela would visit the U.S., hundreds of requests for appearances were submitted. The eight cities that were finally named as stopovers were chosen to serve various purposes. New York City, Los Angeles and Washington were foregone conclusions: three centers of money, clout and glitter that had sizable black communities. Boston was chosen because Senator Edward Kennedy had extended an invitation to Mandela while he was still in jail. Atlanta was included so that Mandela could visit the grave of Martin Luther King Jr. Detroit, Miami and Oakland offered opportunities to pay respects to the labor unions that had been staunch supporters of the antiapartheid movement.

Mandela's arrival in America on June 20, 1990, created a sensation. His magnetism was palpable: this inspiring black hero fired the pride of African Americans, while his willingness to offer years of his life for an unimpeachable cause—and the lack of bitterness he now expressed for those who had imprisoned him—made him the subject of sermons and prayers in churches throughout the land. Mandela also seemed to touch a deep desire in the psyche of Americans both black and white for a leader who might rekindle the biracial civil-rights coalition that had brought down segregation, their country's version of apartheid, a generation before, only to fall apart during the long, hot, riotous summers of the late 1960s.

Mandela's 12-day U.S. visit began in New York City. For one brief, wistful moment, a metropolis that had been pounded by a series of violent racial incidents in recent months

Triumphal tour *Harlem residents awaited an appearance on Mandela's first stop in the U.S., New York City*

seemed to vibrate with one voice shouting "Mandela!" More than 750,000 people lined the streets of lower Manhattan as Mandela sped by in a bulletproof glass chamber borne on a flatbed truck, Vatican-style. At a rally on the steps of city hall, the former prisoner was presented with the key to the city by Mayor David Dinkins, one of five African-American mayors who welcomed him on his trip. As night fell, the top of the Empire State Building was illuminated by spotlights in the black, gold and green colors of the A.N.C. flag.

The next day, Mandela captivated more than 3,000 people gathered at Riverside Church by joining in an exuberant rendition of the *toyi-toyi,* the South African dance of celebration. That night 100,000 people jammed Harlem's Africa Square, content to gaze at the visiting hero whose voice could barely be heard over a feeble public-address system. Later, more than 50,000 listeners cheered Mandela at a rally in Yankee Stadium, where he delighted his audience by donning a baseball cap and declaring, "You now know who I am. I am a Yankee!" Even Mets fans cheered—or so the newspapers reported.

Despite its resemblance to a superstar tour, Mandela's visit to the U.S. had a deeply serious purpose: his objective was to shore up the A.N.C.'s negotiating position as it entered into talks with South African President F.W. de Klerk over the nation's future. Mandela was seeking assurances that the U.S. would not prematurely loosen the economic sanctions it imposed on Pretoria in 1986. He was also looking for "money in buckets" to help the A.N.C. change from a militant underground force to an aboveground political organization. Fund-raising parties in each city would aid that cause: in New York City a $2,500-a-ticket celebration hosted by Eddie Murphy, Spike Lee and Robert De Niro aimed to raise $500,000 from a celebrity crowd that included Paul Newman, Joanne Woodward and Mike Tyson.

Man of the hour *Mandela charmed Americans with his warmth and admiration for their freedoms. Above, he meets with members of the Kennedy family and with President George H.W. Bush. The onetime amateur boxer got a hero's welcome from America's boxing community, including Muhammad Ali, Don King and Mike Tyson*

Like a media-savvy pol—and a single-minded revolutionary—Mandela repeated at every opportunity his call to action: because apartheid was still alive and well, it was too soon to reward Pretoria for its reforms. By one measure his trip was a success before he ever set out. "This is the consolidation of the political credibility of the A.N.C.," declared the Rev. William Howard, past president of the National Council of Churches and a 20-year veteran of the U.S. antiapartheid fight. "Four or five years ago, the very top leadership [of the A.N.C.] couldn't even get a meeting with the person on the Africa desk at the State Department. Now the President has invited Mandela to the White House, and everybody wants to meet with him."

Well, not quite everyone. Mandela's political alliances inevitably drew him into the maelstrom of U.S. politics. Even before he arrived in New York, there were rumblings among American Jews about his praise for the Palestine Liberation Organization: Mandela had met with Yasser Arafat three times since being released from prison in February. In a televised interview, he also had kind words to say about Cuba's Fidel Castro and Libya's Muammar Gaddafi, at the time deeply at odds with the United States. Representative

William Dannemeyer, Republican of California, spoke for a vocal minority when he said that Mandela's past made it "a national disgrace" that he had been invited to address Congress.

Despite such concerns, Mandela was received cordially at the White House by a generally sympathetic President George H.W. Bush, who arranged a formal welcoming ceremony on the White House lawn, a reception generally reserved for heads of state. Mandela's humble official title during his visit to the U.S.—Deputy President of the African National Congress—did not obscure the fact that he clearly represented the future of his nation. The next day he addressed a joint session of Congress, where he was greeted by a standing ovation and interrupted by applause 19 times during his 35-min. speech. After his American journey concluded at a huge outdoor rally in Oakland, TIME declared, "What Bolivar was to South America, what Lincoln was to America, Nelson Mandela is to South Africa: the Liberator." Amid the euphoria, few paused to realize that Mandela had not yet liberated anyone, and that he now faced his greatest challenge: the freeing of all South Africans from centuries of racial bitterness.

Icon *Mandela's U.S. visit was featured on the cover of* TIME's *July 2, 1990, issue*

"Our People Demand Democracy"

Excerpts from Nelson Mandela's address to a joint session of Congress, July 12, 1990:

Mr. Speaker, Mr. President, esteemed members of the United States Congress ... we have come ... into these hallowed chambers of the United States Congress not as pretenders to greatness but as a particle of a people, one we know to be noble and heroic, enduring, multiplying, permanent, rejoicing in the expectation and knowledge that their humanity will be reaffirmed and enlarged by open and unfettered communion with the nations of the world.

We fight for and visualize a future in which all shall, without regard to race, color, creed or sex, have the right to vote and to be voted into all elective organs of state. We are engaged in struggle to ensure that the rights of every individual are guaranteed and protected through a democratic constitution, the rule of law, an entrenched bill of rights, which should be enforced by an independent judiciary as well as a multiparty political system ...

To deny any person their human rights is to challenge their very humanity. To impose on them a wretched life of hunger and deprivation is to dehumanize them. But such has been the terrible fate of all black persons in our country under the system of apartheid ...

We could not have made an acquaintance through literature with human giants such as George Washington, Abraham Lincoln and Thomas Jefferson and not been moved to act as they were moved to act. We could not have heard of and admired John Brown, Sojourner Truth, Frederick Douglass, W.E.B. Du Bois, Marcus Garvey, Martin Luther King Jr. and others ... and not be moved to act as they were moved to act. We could not have known of your Declaration of Independence and not elected to join in the struggle to guarantee the people's life, liberty and the pursuit of happiness ...

The day may not be far when we will borrow the words of Thomas Jefferson and speak of the will of the South African nation ... it must surely be that there will be born a country on the southern tip of Africa which you will be proud to call a friend and an ally because of its contribution to the universal striving towards liberty, human rights, prosperity and peace among the peoples.

Let that day come now ... By our common actions let us ensure that justice triumphs without delay. When that has come to pass, then shall we all be entitled to acknowledge the salute when others say of us, "Blessed are the peacemakers."

All smiles *Nobel laureate Mandela sports his Peace Prize medal in Norway*

Hail to the Peacemaker

■■■■■■

O N NOV. 17, 1993—BLEARY-EYED FROM NEGOTIATIONS OVER FINAL DE-
tails that had dragged on for nine hours past their scheduled conclusion—19
men ascended the podium in a cavernous convention center outside Johannesburg and signed, one by one, a draft constitution designed to remake
completely the nation of South Africa, at last giving equal rights to citizens
of every color. The last-minute delay was nothing to blacks who had waited generations for
this moment. "We have reached the end of an era," declared a triumphant Nelson Mandela, who had led negotiations for the African National Congress. President F.W. de Klerk
agreed, saying, "South Africa will never be the same again."

WALTER DHLADHLA—AFP—GETTY IMAGES

That was the idea. The new law of the land was a package of compromises designed to bring full democracy and a long list of fundamental rights to 28 million increasingly impatient blacks, while assuring 5 million apprehensive whites that black rule would not threaten their lives and livelihoods. The agreement called for elections to be held in April 1994, after which the nation would be governed by a two-house parliament—one elected by proportional representation, the other by nine new provincial legislatures—that would write a permanent constitution. The President, chosen by the winning party, would serve a five-year term and would oversee a Cabinet of 27 ministers, including representatives from any party that won 5% of the vote.

The signing capped a long, contentious process of negotiation that was marred by hostility between the A.N.C. and De Klerk's government. And even as the political leaders clashed, violence among various racial factions had threatened to doom the process. In the interval between the signing of the agreement and the election, the wider world paused to recognize the achievement of the two men who had led this historic rapprochement, Mandela and De Klerk. Few doubted that their commitment to finding a peaceful end to decades of apartheid had averted a long-feared racial bloodbath in their land.

The first honor was given by the Nobel Committee in Sweden, which declared Mandela and De Klerk the winners of the Peace Prize for 1993. For Mandela, the renowned award had special meaning: the Nobel Committee had previously awarded the honor to two leaders in the long struggle against apartheid, former A.N.C. head Albert Luthuli (1960), a Zulu; and Mandela's longtime supporter, Anglican Archbishop Desmond Tutu (1984).

The prize citation recognized the men's "work for the peaceful termination of the apartheid regime, and for laying the foundations for a new democratic South Africa ... By looking ahead to South African reconciliation instead of back at the deep wounds of the past, they have shown personal integrity and great personal courage."

While Mandela and De Klerk were in Norway in December 1993 to receive their award, the men were visited by the editors of TIME, who had decided to name them two of the magazine's four Men of the Year, 1993. TIME's annual recognition of an individual's impact on history also included another pair of bitter enemies who had reached a settlement over the future of their angry and suspicious peoples, Israel's President Yitzhak Rabin and Palestine Liberation Organization leader Yasser Arafat.

Speaking with the two South African leaders, TIME's editors quickly realized the extent to which their long months of negotiation had left them distrustful of one another. As the magazine delicately put it, "Mandela and De Klerk perfectly meet the first precondition of peacemakers: they do not like each other very much. Neither one, in the season of their triumphs, seems grateful for the gift of the other. But those triumphs are immense. These unlikely allies created the conditions for an event the world could not have foreseen only a few years earlier."

In the months to come, these two men would contend for the presidency of South Africa in the first national elections in which all citizens would vote. But for a few brief moments before they would tangle at the polls, this unlikely team of partners—one the son of a Xhosa nobleman who spent 27 years in jail as a prisoner of conscience, the other a fourth-generation Afrikaner and hence a lifelong beneficiary of white privilege—stood smiling in history's spotlight, and rightly so.

Making history *Mandela and De Klerk, along with Mideast leaders Yitzhak Rabin and Yasser Arafat, were named Men of the Year 1993 by* TIME. *Rabin and Arafat signed the Oslo Accords at the White House in September 1993*

"We Took the Right Turn"

In December 1993, TIME *writers and editors conducted a joint interview with Nelson Mandela and F.W. de Klerk, weeks before naming the two Men of the Year for their work in ending apartheid. Here are excerpts from that provocative session.*

Mandela I found Mr. De Klerk very positive, very bright, very confident of himself, and ready to accommodate the views I expressed. The National Party had announced a [reform] program in which they talked about "group rights." I said to him, "Look, this will introduce apartheid through the back door." He replied, "Well, if you don't like it, then we'll scrap it." I smuggled a message to the A.N.C. leadership in Zambia and said, "I think we can do business with this man." I did not expect that he was going to be so positive.

De Klerk I don't believe I am irreplaceable. I don't believe he is irreplaceable. The fact is … we were the leaders.

Mandela I was disappointed by him because he did things that I did not expect. Such as the question of violence. I said to him that if there is anything that will create bad blood between us, it is the slaughter of human beings with government connivance. That is the one thing that has created a great deal of friction between me and De Klerk.

De Klerk A different approach from the A.N.C. could have prevented much of the grief. Mandela could have started negotiating sooner. They should never have embarked on acts of terrorism, killing innocent civilians; it had a dramatic effect on white public opinion. Sanctions were quite counterproductive. They built a strong sense of nationalism: We will not allow the world to tell us what to do!

Mandela Armed struggle must be intended to hit at the symbols of oppression and not to slaughter human beings.

De Klerk America is the only exception where the melting pot works. In the rest of the world, nation-states that have clear majorities of one ethnic group within the country have been the pattern. When apartheid started, the colonial powers weren't worried about black political rights at all. In America racial discrimination was thriving.

Mandela The government did not want any form of demonstration from blacks, no matter how disciplined, how peaceful. Any demonstration was regarded as a declaration of war against white supremacy.

De Klerk I don't think it was a good idea to tell people where to live and to kick people out of particular townships. It became forced removals [into Bantustan homelands]. That is where apartheid became morally unjustifiable. As it failed, it became more and more racist and less and less morally defensible. People's dignity was being impaired, and it brought humiliation. I have said time and again, "We are sorry that that happened."

Mandela I don't think it is necessary for De Klerk to apologize. It is what a person does to ensure that the most brutal system of racial oppression is completely eliminated from our society. There is no doubt that South Africans, black and white, are coming together. I have been addressing some of the most conservative sectors. Their response is so positive. One of the first questions is, "When did you change your policy?" I say, "This has always been our policy."

De Klerk I would hope that history would recognize that I, together with all those who supported me, have shown courage, integrity, honesty at the moment of truth in our history. That we took the right turn.

Mandela In spite of my criticism, it must be acknowledged he has made a very important contribution to the transformation of an apartheid state to a nonracial society.

Odd couple *The Nobel laureates share a photo-op. Even during the Peace Prize ceremonies, the bitter legacy of apartheid cast a shadow: when Mandela and De Klerk appeared jointly on an Oslo hotel balcony, some activists in the crowd jeered at De Klerk, shouting "Kill the Boer!"*

"Let a New Age Dawn!"

Excerpts from remarks by Nelson Mandela upon receiving the Nobel Prize for Peace, Dec. 10, 1993.

I extend my heartfelt thanks to the Norwegian Nobel Committee for elevating us to the status of a Nobel Peace Prize winner.

I would also like to take this opportunity to congratulate my compatriot and fellow laureate, State President F.W. de Klerk, on his receipt of this high honor.

Together, we join two distinguished South Africans, the late Chief Albert Luthuli and His Grace Archbishop Desmond Tutu, to whose seminal contributions to the peaceful struggle against the evil system of apartheid you paid well-deserved tribute by awarding them the Nobel Peace Prize.

It will not be presumptuous of us if we also add, among our predecessors, the name of another outstanding Nobel Peace Prize winner, the late Rev. Martin Luther King Jr.

He, too, grappled with and died in the effort to make a contribution to the just solution of the same great issues of the day which we have had to face as South Africans ...

We stand here today as nothing more than a representative of the millions of our people who dared to rise up against a social system whose very essence is war, violence, racism, oppression, repression and the impoverishment of an entire people.

I am also here today as a representative of the millions of people across the globe, the antiapartheid movement, the governments and organizations that joined with us, not to fight against South Africa as a country or any of its peoples, but to oppose an inhuman system and sue for a speedy end to the apartheid crime against humanity.

These countless human beings, both inside and outside our country, had the nobility of spirit to stand in the path of tyranny and injustice, without seeking selfish gain. They recognised that an injury to one is an injury to all and therefore acted together in defense of justice and a common human decency.

Because of their courage and persistence for many years,

we can, today, even set the dates when all humanity will join together to celebrate one of the outstanding human victories of our century.

When that moment comes, we shall, together, rejoice in a common victory over racism, apartheid and white minority rule ...

The value of our shared reward will and must be measured by the joyful peace which will triumph, because the common humanity that bonds both black and white into one human race will have said to each one of us that we shall all live like the children of paradise.

Thus shall we live, because we will have created a society which recognizes that all people are born equal, with each entitled in equal measure to life, liberty, prosperity, human rights and good governance. Such a society should never allow again that there should be prisoners of conscience nor that any person's human right should be violated.

Neither should it ever happen that once more the avenues to peaceful change are blocked by usurpers who seek to take power away from the people, in pursuit of their own, ignoble purposes ...

Moved by that appeal and inspired by the eminence you have thrust upon us, we undertake that we too will do what we can to contribute to the renewal of our world so that none should, in future, be described as the "wretched of the earth."

Let the strivings of us all prove Martin Luther King Jr. to have been correct, when he said that humanity can no longer be tragically bound to the starless midnight of racism and war.

Let the efforts of us all prove that he was not a mere dreamer when he spoke of the beauty of genuine brotherhood and peace being more precious than diamonds or silver or gold. Let a new age dawn!

Winds of change *Mandela, once a phantom without a face in his own nation, mugged his way through his triumphant 1994 election run*

Let My People Vote

WHITE-HAIRED, BEARDED CRONJE TSHAKA WAS STANDING IN A long line outside the polling station in Guguletu, one of the toughest and grimiest of the black townships around Cape Town, when a TIME reporter asked the elder's age. Tshaka replied that he was 95—older than the 82-year-old African National Congress. Now, on April 27, 1994, Tshaka was about to outlive apartheid. Clutching his passbook in one hand and his cane in the other, Tshaka was waiting patiently in line to vote—like all South Africa's black citizens, for the first time in his life. He shook off offers of help and walked unsteadily but unaided into the polling station. Minutes later he emerged, a broad grin lighting his face. "I never thought I would see this day," he said.

That sentiment resounded around the world, as TV viewers watched events many had never dared to imagine they might witness. In a series of astonishing episodes, the old South Africa of segregation and oppression dissolved and re-emerged as a tentatively hopeful, newly democratic nation. On April 27 the old order formally ended as cheering crowds in the nine new provincial capitals hailed the lowering of apartheid's blue-white-and-orange flag and the raising of a banner with six colors symbolizing the people, their blood, their land, the gold under the ground, the sky—and white for peace. At the same moment, the country became whole again. The 10 bogus black Bantustans, designed by apartheid architects as places of exile for people with black skin, were abolished. The armed services became the South African National Defense Force and would soon begin to absorb former enemies from guerrilla armies like the A.N.C.'s Spear of the Nation, founded by Nelson Mandela.

Perhaps predictably, a group of bloody-minded white rightists had tried—and failed—to disrupt the process of change. They launched a campaign of small bombings against railways, power lines and A.N.C. offices in the conservative farm region west of Johannesburg. The week before the election, they detonated powerful car bombs in downtown Johannesburg, in neighboring Germiston and at the international airport, killing a total of 21 people and injuring more than 150. The police rounded up 34 suspects, all members of the Afrikaner Resistance Movement, whose insignia deliberately aped a swastika.

PETER TURNLEY—CORBIS

Dawn of a new era *In April 1994, blacks formed a queue to vote for the first time in the Transkei, Nelson Mandela's home region. The balloting was extended from three to four days to accommodate the late-entering Inkatha Freedom Party*

On the hustings *Mandela, wearing one of his trademark batik "Madiba" shirts, charms a crowd in Soweto*

Voters, especially blacks eager to embrace the day of their liberation, were not deterred. The election to name a five-year government of national unity was astonishingly peaceful. Lines of determined voters stretched a mile and more at polling places. Many polls opened hours late; some ran out of ballots as well as the invisible ink used to mark the hands of those who had already made their choice. While exasperated thousands waited, election workers gave puzzled first-timers impromptu lessons in how to mark a ballot. One problem: the ballots, printed weeks before, did not include the last-minute entry in the race, the Zulu-led Inkatha Freedom Party, and had to be updated with paste-on stickers. To ensure fairness, Inkatha's boss, Zulu Chief Mangosuthu Buthelezi, who had long claimed he would not take part in the election, demanded—and eventually received—a fourth day of voting.

The surprise was not that the election was carried out well but that it happened at all. Here was a white government, still with a monopoly grip on political power, handing over control of the country. Those whites and their forebears had methodically segregated blacks, paid them a pittance, ignored their needs and barely pretended to educate them. Now, by agreement, the whites stepped back and yielded power to that eager but ill-prepared majority.

FOUR HARROWING YEARS

That new beginning was the capstone of an extraordinary four years in the history of South Africa, beginning with Mandela's release from prison. It was achieved only through long, painful negotiations that broke down again and again amid mutual recriminations, even as the nation spiraled into violence and strife. In fact, the four years that followed Mandela's release were by far the bloodiest of the apartheid era. Some 15,000 South Africans were killed in that period—the vast majority of them victims not of fighting between whites and blacks but between the supporters of the A.N.C. and Buthelezi's Inkatha Freedom Party.

Zulu power *Members of the Inkatha Freedom Party demonstrate in the streets during the 1994 election*

Many people contributed to make the nation's first free elections a success, but no one denied that only one person had the standing with a broad range of South Africans to forge a deal, against all obstacles: Nelson Mandela. Those obstacles were formidable. Mandela had to struggle against the hatreds aroused by his nation's history of racial segregation and prejudice, quelling both blacks' bitterness over apartheid and whites' fears of retribution if blacks came into power. He had to convert the A.N.C.—for decades an imperiled, outlawed organization with many of its key leaders in prison—into a viable, respectable political party. He had to battle concerns over the A.N.C.'s association with socialists and communists, as well as his own outdated beliefs in the promise of Marxism, whose influence had receded around the world during his long incarceration. And he had to fight all these battles while his personal life was under an unwelcome spotlight due to the ongoing trials and scandals surrounding his wife Winnie, and his marriage was dissolving *(see following chapter)*.

1990: Descent into Bloodshed

De Klerk's 1990 decision to release Mandela put the future of South Africa into play, and in the months that followed, every political group in the nation began angling to control its destiny. Some die-hard Afrikaners joined extremist paramilitary organizations like the Afrikaner Resistance Movement, whose attempts to derail a settlement would reach a peak in June 1993, when hundreds of its members broke into the negotiating venue near Johannesburg, yelling racist epithets, trashing offices and even urinating in the council chambers.

But the nation's most compelling problem was black-on-black violence, centering on the Zulus and Buthelezi, whose relationship with Mandela was long and complex. Buthelezi had stood by Mandela during his early days in prison, and Mandela—the walking embodiment of a man with a long memory—never forgot that. But over the decades, the ferociously anticommunist Buthelezi had become a major opponent of the A.N.C. and the darling of those who feared the A.N.C.'s Marxist connections, such as British Prime Minister Margaret Thatcher. In July 1990 he retooled the Inkatha Freedom Party he had founded in 1975 into a serious political party, intending it to serve as an alternative to the A.N.C. as a potential black ruling party.

That summer, Zulu and A.N.C. paramilitary groups began clashing all around the country, especially in the Zulu stronghold province of KwaZulu-Natal. As the body count mounted in a series of gruesome massacres and necklacings, Mandela sought to reach out personally to Buthelezi, but grudge-bearing A.N.C. senior officials refused to hear of it. "They nearly throttled me," Mandela said. Across South Africa in 1990, blacks fought and killed each other with ferocity. In many cases, white policemen stood by, letting blood spill, aware that the images of blacks killing blacks sent a strong message to the world that South Africa's native peoples were far from ready to govern themselves—and that even Mandela couldn't control them.

1991-93: Breakdowns and Breakthroughs

The eruptions of violence seemed timed to stymie the negotiating process, and Mandela began to believe that the attacks were the result of a "third force" within the state security organization acting in collusion with ministers within De Klerk's government. In April 1991 the A.N.C. suspended negotiations with the government. Three months later newspapers published documents proving that the security police had indeed been financing the Inkatha party through secret bank accounts. Much later, investigations revealed that rogue elements in De Klerk's government had trained Inkatha assassins and encouraged the black-on-black violence.

The revelations shook De Klerk's government: heads rolled, and De Klerk called for a national peace conference in September 1991. Both Mandela and Buthelezi attended, but the effort at restoring goodwill failed when the notoriously erratic Buthelezi pointedly refused to shake the hand of either De Klerk or Mandela at the meeting's televised conclusion. Yet Mandela and De Klerk were determined to press ahead, and the first formal meetings to hammer out a plan for the nation's post-apartheid future began in December.

As talks stalled, Mandela came to suspect that the government's plan in releasing him had been nothing more than a ploy intended to calm the nation's blacks, while offering them only a token presence in the government. He took the podium to charge that De Klerk, even as head of "an illegitimate, discredited, minority regime ... had certain standards to uphold." Relations between the two grew icy: they did not speak, even by telephone, for six months.

Despite the setback, in March 1992 De Klerk succeeded in getting 68% of the nation's all-white voters to approve the creation of a new constitution—a strong sign that they knew apartheid's days were numbered. One month later, the nation convulsed again when the charismatic Chris Hani, a leader of the M.K. militant wing of the A.N.C. and a top official in the South African Communist Party, was gunned down in cold blood by a white man. As fears of widespread bloodshed mounted, De Klerk appealed to Mandela to calm the nation. Mandela agreed, and he noted in his televised remarks that the assassin was a racist Polish immigrant who had been nabbed quickly thanks to a tip provided to police by an Afrikaner woman. The nation heeded his pleas for calm and remained generally quiet. Mandela had never seemed more presidential, De Klerk never more powerless.

In the months that followed, the two leaders' deputies—A.N.C. secretary-general Cyril Ramaphosa and government minister Roelof Meyer—continued meeting and managed to reach a

The winner *An exultant Mandela delights his supporters at a victory rally by busting out in a buoyant* toyi-toyi *dance*

crucial transitional agreement: after its first free elections, South Africa would establish a government of national unity for five years, in which all parties would serve. Ramaphosa sealed the deal by agreeing to guarantee previously promised retirement pensions for white bureaucrats. The compromise offered an opportunity for whites to get used to the notion of black voters and black government ministers—and for blacks to prove themselves capable of ruling.

With impetus restored to the negotiations, Mandela and De Klerk met again in November 1993 and hammered out a final deal. Mandela held off De Klerk's poorly camouflaged attempts to impose a white veto over the proceedings of the proposed unity government. In return, Mandela agreed to maintain a degree of limited autonomy for the nation's provinces, a sop to the fears of both white voters and the Zulus. On Nov. 19, 1993, the men at last announced that all South Africans would vote to elect a new government in April 1994, at which time the apartheid constitution would give way to a new constitution promising equal rights for all—and blacks like Cronje Tshaka would exchange their passbooks for a ballot.

The election campaign was an anticlimax: no one doubted that Mandela would trounce De Klerk. If not a great orator, Mandela, now 75, proved adept at the one-on-one wooing of voters, energetically hamming his way through photo ops, kissing babies, donning tribal garb and showing off his graceful dance moves. The excitement in the campaign was provided by Buthelezi, who at first declared that Inkatha would not take part and demanded that Zulus be allowed to form their own nation. But sensing he was moving against history's tide and might be marginalized, he joined the process a week before the election began, necessitating the production of new ballots and a one-day voting extension in some areas. When the results were announced, Nelson Mandela and the A.N.C. party had won 62% of the vote; De Klerk's National Party received 20%; Buthelezi's Inkatha Freedom Party garnered 10%. For the first time in South Africa's history, the people—all the people—had spoken.

Winnie's Woes

LIKE THE FREEDOM FIGHTER SHE MARRIED, NOMZAMO WINIFRED MADIKI-zela was marked from birth with a name that said much about her future: in Xhosa, Nomzamo translates loosely as "one who perseveres in the face of trials and tribulations." And persevere Winnie Mandela did—showing a brave face amid decades apart from her husband, constant harassment by her government and threats against her life. Yet many of her trials, including the multiple criminal inquiries that severely tarnished her reputation in later years, were the result of her own failings.

Nelson Mandela's second wife was born the sixth of 11 children of a missionary schoolteacher in 1936. She was raised in the village of Bizana in the Transkei; her father was especially cold and aloof, and she developed a reputation for being willful. Like Mandela, she came to Johannesburg in her 20s; the social worker went through a whirlwind courtship with the divorced activist, who was 13 years her senior when they married in 1958. Only 26 years old when Mandela was sentenced to life in prison, Winnie was left alone to raise two daughters, with the added strain of constant surveillance and harassment by government security services.

Eventually these tensions would drive her to excessive drinking and a string of alleged extramarital affairs. Still, she found time not only to nurture her family but also to champion the fight against apartheid. Her visits were the only bright spots in her husband's first years in jail, and she played a major role in focusing attention on his plight. For decades she electrified A.N.C. rallies as the stand-in for the movement's outlawed leader. Detained several times under the Terrorism Act, Winnie was banished to the remote town of Brandfort in 1977; the period in exile was especially difficult. She defied the security forces by returning to Soweto in 1985 to lead antiapartheid rallies. The next year, she shocked many A.N.C. supporters when she declared at a rally, "With our boxes of matches and our necklaces, we shall liberate this country." That sort of rhetoric—not to mention the grisly execution by incineration it endorsed—was precisely the sort of black-on-black violence the white regime was eager to promote and her imprisoned husband was doing his best, from behind bars, to stop.

In the late 1980s, Winnie gathered around her a circle of thuggish bodyguards, known as the Mandela United Football Club, who happily roughed up anyone who aroused her displeasure. In 1989, the body of a murdered 13-year-old black boy, Stompie M. Seipei—suspected by her allies of being a police informant—was found in her home, leading to charges of murder, assault and kidnapping. Her husband's release from prison the next year put Winnie in the world spotlight. Yet their reunion was strained—reports of her alleged infidelities and excesses had reached Mandela in jail, and the two, who had spent barely a few days together in 27 years, were essentially strangers. Winnie's 1991 trial in the Stompie affair resulted in a conviction on a kidnapping charge with a suspended sentence; more serious counts were dismissed or resulted in acquittals. Her husband gamely appeared at the trial each day, even as he negotiated with the regime on the nation's future. In 1992 the two declared they would separate.

Winnie was now a political force in her own right, and when Mandela became President in 1994, she was appointed Deputy Minister for Arts, Culture, Science and Technology. But her constant criticism of her estranged husband's government led to her ouster a year later. The two divorced in 1996; during the trial, the always reserved Mandela told the court that his wife had made him "the loneliest man" after his release from prison. The following year, Winnie appeared before the nation's Truth and Reconciliation Commission to respond to charges arising from the reign of terror conducted in her name in the late 1980s. Commission chair Archbishop Desmond Tutu implored her, "I beg you, I beg you, I beg you—You are a great person, and you don't know how your greatness would be enhanced if you were to say: 'Sorry. Things went wrong. Forgive me.'" Winnie remained unmoved, declaring herself blameless. The tribunal concluded that she was aware of—and likely participated in—several crimes and was directly "responsible for committing … gross violations of human rights."

Winnie's imperious nature by now was manifesting itself in a lavish lifestyle that led some critics to call her "South Africa's Evita." In 2001 she faced new charges: 85 counts of fraud, including the alleged embezzlement of $100,000 from the A.N.C. Women's League, of which she was then president. Convicted in 2003, she was sentenced to five years in jail. The penalty was later reduced to a fine and suspended sentence by an appeals court. She was shunned by Thabo Mbeki, Mandela's successor as President, and by the A.N.C. he led. But as campaigning geared up in 2008 to elect Mbeki's successor, Winnie surprised observers by declaring she would run for Parliament on the A.N.C. ticket, and at the party conference in March 2009, she was the top vote-getter for the A.N.C.'s National Executive Committee, leading to predictions she would be named to new President Jacob Zuma's cabinet. That did not occur, but it seemed that at the age of 73, Winnie Madikizela Mandela had succeeded in putting many of the messier details of her past behind her. She remains immensely popular among many impoverished South Africans, who continue to refer to her as "the mother of the nation."

A New Era Begins

■■ ▬ ▬▬

N EVER, NEVER AND NEVER AGAIN SHALL THIS BEAUTIFUL LAND experience the oppression of one by another," Nelson Mandela proclaimed in his inaugural address on May 10, 1994, the highlight of a joyous celebration attended by representatives of more than 150 nations. To thunderous applause, South Africa's first black President concluded his address by pledging that his country would no longer "suffer the indignity of being the skunk of the world," and he declared, "Let freedom reign. The sun shall never set on so glorious a human achievement!"

Mandela's ascent to the highest office in South Africa was a political miracle that exceeded the wildest hopes of apartheid's foes. Yet it also marked the moment when the primary author of that miracle began to descend from the mythic realm of moral heroism and enter the real world of politics, a world not of ethical absolutes but of compromises and uncertainties. What Mario Cuomo observed about politicians in democracy—that they campaign in poetry but govern in prose—was especially true for Mandela, who aroused enormous expectations. Some of these would be surpassed, others realized in part, and still others would become the subject of bitter disappointment.

The challenges facing Mandela were considerable. The country's economy, suffering from sanctions, had been stagnant for five years. More than 12 million people had no easy access to clean water, while more than half the nation's households had no electricity, and the health-care system, especially for blacks, was a shambles. Compounding the difficulty, the military, civil service, police and judiciary were all staffed exclusively by white men. Yet these woes paled beside the ongoing bitterness of the racial conflicts that had claimed untold thousands of lives in the years under apartheid.

The challenge was magnified by the inexperience of the new team. Seasoned by decades of battling apartheid in resistance, A.N.C. members were ill-prepared for the complex task of governing; they remained more a liberation movement than a genuine political party. Yet however unprepared for his new office, Mandela soon displayed the restraint and inclusiveness that would become the signature of his presidency. He formed a coalition government with his former jailers, F.W. de Klerk's National Party, and declared that white soldiers, police officers and civil servants would all be given job security to ensure national stability. Three months into his tenure, Mandela announced that "the government of national unity set itself

Road warrior *Mandela arrives in France in 1996 on a jet bearing the new flag of South Africa. During his term as President, he traveled widely to represent his reborn nation and seek investment in its struggling economy*

two interrelated tasks: reconciliation and reconstruction, nation building and development."

The first of these goals was advanced by Mandela's single greatest accomplishment as President. A year after taking office, he collaborated with the respected Archbishop Desmond Tutu to establish the Truth and Reconciliation Commission. Charged with investigating the human-rights abuses of the apartheid era, the commission was given the power to grant amnesty to those who confessed. In a farsighted initiative that greatly relieved white fears of racial witch hunts and campaigns for revenge, Mandela insisted the commission also investigate abuses by the A.N.C. The policy so infuriated some of Mandela's erstwhile supporters that the A.N.C. attempted to suppress publication of the commission's final report in 1999, which recorded the group's investigations of more than 7,000 cases of alleged human-rights violations. Through this body, Mandela succeeded in making the willingness of each side to offer and accept forgiveness something close to a patriotic duty and helped heal his land.

REBUILDING

If reconciliation was difficult, reconstruction was even more daunting. Mandela pledged upon taking office to redistribute a third of South Africa's fertile agricultural lands to black farmers, but he later abandoned this promise when it proved beyond the government's ability to implement. Another promise, to build more than 1 million new homes for South Africa's poor, met with greater, if still incomplete, success. By the time Mandela left office in 1999, about 60% of that number of houses had been built or were under construction. He could take pride in a number of successes: during his presidency, drinkable water came to the homes of more than 3 million people, electricity to an additional 2 million and telephone service to 1.3 million, while the government renovated more than 1,500 schools.

Mandela helped South Africa become one nation, but he could not make it indivisible. The nation's schools remained stubbornly segregated. In the negotiations that created the new government, the white parties insisted upon a concession that would allow schoolchildren to be taught in the language of their choice. As a result, each school was conducted in only one of South Africa's 11 official languages, many of them tribal. The result was a deeply segregated system in which the persistent disparity in wealth between black African and white Afrikaner families meant that their schools were not only separate but stubbornly unequal.

Mandela's critics often charged that he was disengaged from the day-to-day mechanics of governing, an allegation he seldom took the trouble to deny. Instead, he often reminded supporters and critics alike that he had never wanted to be President, primarily because of his advanced age (he was 75 when he took office). By 1997, he had largely handed over administrative responsibility to his heir apparent, Thabo Mbeki, so that he could focus his energies on the kind of moral leadership that nobody else could provide. When the govern-

Citizen of the World

Libya
Mandela drew fire by reaching out to Libya's Muammar Gaddafi, but his gambit paid off in a settlement that brought the bombers of Pan Am Flight 103 to justice.

China
Mandela confers with President Jiang Zemin of China in Beijing in 1999. In addition to the nations shown here, Mandela visited India, Canada, France, Italy, Saudi Arabia and many more during his presidency.

Britain
Mandela and Queen Elizabeth II became good friends during his repeated visits to the United Kingdom. Here, Mandela visits in July 1996. But he refused to meet with former P.M. and A.N.C. adversary Margaret Thatcher.

The U.S.
Mandela raises his fist in a black-power salute in 1996 with an unusual ally, Strom Thurmond, the Senator from South Carolina who for decades strongly opposed racial integration in the U.S.

Teamwork *Mandela awards rugby's World Cup to Francois Pienaar, captain of South Africa's national team, in 1995. "When he handed me the Cup," Pienaar recalled, "he said, 'Thank you very much for what you've done for South Africa.' And I said 'No, you've got it wrong. Actually, it's what you've done.'" At right, Mandela visits the home of one of his former jailers from his days in Victor Verster prison*

ment ran out of money for improving health care in the countryside, for example, he raised funds from South Africa's business community to build more than 500 new clinics.

INSPIRER-IN-CHIEF

Mandela best served South Africans during his presidency when he harnessed his mythic status to the country's needs. South Africa's ambassador to the world traveled tirelessly to drum up interest and investment in a reborn nation that badly needed both. He was also instrumental in helping Libya's longtime outlaw leader, Muammar Gaddafi, reconnect with the West, helping negotiate a settlement that allowed the Libyan intelligence agents accused of conspiring to bomb Pan Am Flight 103 in December 1988 to be tried in the Netherlands.

Mandela also set an example at home, astonishing observers by seeking out his former Afrikaner prison guards to mend fences, often welcomed as a guest in their homes. At times he seemed to physically embody national unity, as in June 1995, when he presented the rugby World Cup trophy to South Africa's team after its upset victory over New Zealand. Mandela had led blacks in uniting behind the largely white squad and its slogan "One team, one country." When the beaming President walked onto the field wearing a jersey bearing captain Francois Pienaar's number, 72,000 South African spectators in the stadium exploded as one.

Mandela's moral credentials were also bolstered by his frequent public scoldings of both whites and blacks: he urged whites to use their wealth and education for the betterment of the entire nation, and he warned blacks against abusing their newfound majority status. He routinely received standing ovations from the audiences he both chided and charmed. At the end of his five-year term in 1999, he happily handed leadership of the A.N.C. to Mbeki. In one of his last addresses to legislators, Mandela said, "the long walk is not yet over. The prize of a better life has yet to be won." Yet during his presidency, the first steps on that walk were taken and the struggle for that prize was well begun.

The Lion in Winter

■ ▬ ▬

A LTHOUGH NELSON MANDELA LEFT THE LEADERSHIP OF SOUTH Africa to a new generation on June 16, 1999, leadership never left him. From the day he stepped down as South Africa's President at age 80, he confronted a question faced by few other figures in history: How does one retire from being the world's most revered icon of social justice? In the years that followed, the answer turned out to be: One doesn't, not entirely. Mandela's pedestal was not equipped with a ladder.

Even in the twilight of his life, the tall, stooped, increasingly frail old man remained a beacon of conscience, the voice South Africans waited to hear on national problems and the world paid heed to on such global issues as the AIDS epidemic in Africa and the U.S. intervention in Iraq. "He's the one who fought for us," Leocardia Mchunu, a Cape Town child-care worker told TIME in 2004. She, like many other South Africans, said she was voting for the African National Congress (A.N.C.) in that year's election primarily because of her loyalty to Mandela.

He kept busy, yet after 1999 Mandela increasingly found time to savor the private life that was denied to him both in prison and the presidency. While still in office, he had struck up a correspondence with Graça Machel, widow of Mozambique's President Samora Machel, a longtime Mandela supporter who died in an airplane crash in 1986, as regional battles over apartheid were at a peak. Mandela and Machel's exchange of letters soon blossomed into a close friendship, which filled the void left by Mandela's estrangement and eventual divorce from his second wife, Winnie. "At first we enjoyed sharing and having someone to talk to who understood," Machel would remember later. "He would call me often. But our relationship quickly developed into something much deeper. Soon this was no longer a friendship." They were married in July 1998 on Mandela's 80th birthday. "Late in life, I am blooming like a flower because of the love and support she has given me," he would say later.

As a private citizen, Mandela found time to work on causes he felt he had neglected during his presidency, especially AIDS, the plague that has ravaged Africa more than any other continent. He would later describe his refusal to address this issue during his presidential

Sweethearts *Denied personal relationships for more than a quarter-century by his stint in prison, Mandela found happiness in later life with Graça Machel; here they pose for a photo at home after their marriage in 1998*

campaign and term in office as his single greatest regret, citing a lack of moral courage. "I wanted to win, and I didn't talk about AIDS," he told the *Times* of London in 2003. "Africans don't want to talk about it … I could see I was offending my audience. They were horrified."

Now, no longer concerned with opinion polls, Mandela made up for lost time, becoming a tireless advocate for making education, prevention and affordable drugs available to South Africans confronting the disease. "We must not continue debating, to be arguing when people are dying," he told a South African newspaper early in 2002, soon after his successor, Thabo Mbeki, had publicly questioned the link between HIV and AIDS. The lapse haunted Mandela in an intensely personal way; he announced in January 2005 that the recent death of his 54-year-old son Makgotho had been from AIDS, tearfully imploring all South Africans to treat AIDS "like a normal illness" and not something for which "people will go to hell and not to heaven." With such celebrity colleagues as U2 frontman Bono and British musician Dave Stewart, he lent his support to a campaign—dubbed 46664, after his number in prison—which raised money through music for the Global Fund for AIDS.

Mandela also traveled the world, especially the Middle East, Europe and Africa, deploying his moral weight to address conflicts. He spent much of 2001 trying to negotiate an end to the civil war in Burundi and succeeded in setting up a transitional administration to share power between Tutsi and Hutu, although the war continued. The following year he joined with his jailer and emancipator, former South African President F.W. de Klerk, to urge a compromise between Israeli and Palestinian leaders, invoking his nation's example of peaceful transition from confrontation to partnership, but the effort was largely ignored. It was a rare failure, for Mandela's voice was impossible to ignore, even if it was dismissed by some leaders. In the months leading up to the 2003 U.S. intervention in Iraq, Mandela described George W. Bush as a "President who has no foresight, who cannot think properly."

As he aged, Mandela's frailty became more apparent. He grew tired more easily and occasionally became short tempered. In 2000, he underwent radiation therapy for prostate cancer, which sent the disease into remission. His doctors insisted he rest more often; he did so by spending time with his new wife and his many grandchildren. Denied the chance to see his own children grow up, he now doted on their offspring: one, Ndileka Mandela, lovingly described him to TIME in 2004 as "a sweet pensioner."

In June of that same year Mandela announced that he would scale back his non-stop public schedule. "When I told one of my advisers a few months ago that I wanted to retire," Mandela said at a news conference, "he growled at me: 'You *are* retired.' If that is really the case, then I should say I now announce that I am retiring from retirement." Even so, in 2007 Mandela joined a new group of experienced statesmen, the Elders, who proposed to offer their counsel and wisdom to troubled areas of the globe. On June 27, 2008, tens of thousands gathered in London's Hyde Park for a concert celebrating Mandela's 90th birthday.

By that time Thabo Mbeki's government had become so deeply troubled that Mbeki stepped down early from his second term as president. Mandela supported the party's choice for his replacement, the controversial Jacob Zuma, electrifying a Johannesburg crowd when he appeared at a campaign rally for Zuma in April 2009. As the nation weathered a stormy passage, Mandela's heritage became the focus of fresh debate. He may have united us, went an argument that found wide currency in South Africa, but perhaps he set the country up for disappointment. Ongoing edgy racial relations made his rainbow vision seem ever more

Golden years *At top left, Mandela and Archbishop Desmond Tutu celebrate after South Africa was chosen to host soccer's World Cup tournament in 2010. Both wear "Madiba shirts," named after Mandela's widely used honorific. Top right, Mandela appears at a 2009 rally for A.N.C. candidate Jacob Zuma. At bottom, he is honored by his Xhosa tribe for his service in 2004, as King Sigcawu places a leopard-skin crown on his head*

illusory. "Whites eagerly embraced Mandela, but not the race from which he came," political consultant Aubrey Matshiqi told Time. "The Mandela era created the delusion of a rainbow nation, which masked a lot of the problems between black and white people in this country." Yet even Matshiqi had to admit, "There's an aura about him … The first time I saw him, I actually wanted to cry and I don't know why."

Journalist Charlene Smith, who wrote one of the dozens of books about Mandela, understood this feeling. "South Africa was a nation of abused children," she says. "He came in and loved us all." If his last years raised the question about whether it was possible to retire from being Nelson Mandela, the first years without him will pose a different dilemma for his nation: How will its revolution of conscience continue without the revolutionary who led it?

Valedictory

■■■■■

AFTER HIS FORMAL RETIREMENT FROM POLITICS IN 1999, NELSON MANDELA came to inhabit a kind of pop-culture Valhalla: his story, his courage, his grace—all embodied in his beaming, indelible smile—earned him the sort of adulation usually reserved for rock stars, Pontiffs and sports heroes. Everyone, it seemed, from billionaires and dictators to poets and princesses, wanted to express their admiration for the man his countrymen now universally called "Madiba," a Thembu term for a beloved elder.

Mandela artfully deployed his superstar status, using his fame to draw the media spotlight to his favorite causes, most prominently the battle against HIV/AIDS in Africa. Famously self-disciplined, he was unaltered by his global celebrity, and small gestures moved him more than galas and awards. He was thrilled in 2003 when he received a handwritten note on his birthday from a 13-year-old white South African girl who wrote, "You've changed my life for the better. You've taught me to love people of all races and colors." His correspondent was Wilma Verwoerd, great-granddaughter of apartheid architect Hendrik Verwoerd, South Africa's Prime Minister when Mandela was sentenced to life in prison in 1964.

The next year Mandela issued his famous declaration that he was "retiring from retirement," and he began to be seen in public less frequently. He and wife Graça Machel made a spectacular appearance in Johannesburg in July 2010 at the final match of the FIFA World Cup soccer tournament. Waving to the crowd from beneath a fur hat—it was wintertime in the southern hemisphere—Madiba flashed his wonderful smile as tens of thousands cheered and vuvuzelas blared. Yet even this triumphant moment walked hand in hand with sorrow: Mandela's 13-year-old great-granddaughter had been killed in a car accident only hours before the tournament began, and he had missed the competition's opening ceremony as a result.

As the years went by, Mandela's respiratory system began to fail—the result, it was widely speculated, of his years working in the quarry at Robben Island. If so, the past was finally catching up to the man who had always trained his sights on the future. Late in 2012, as Mandela emerged from one of his ever more frequent hospitalizations, Machel admitted that "his spirit and sparkle are fading." As TIME managing editor Richard Stengel reports in the Foreword to this book, Mandela's famed memory also began to fade away in these last years. But the memories he created, the example he set and the generosity of spirit he brought to his vital work of liberation and reconciliation are in no danger of fading away.

Farewell *Mandela's last major public appearance was in July 2010 at the final match of the FIFA World Cup soccer tournament*

"During my lifetime I have dedicated myself to this struggle of the African people. I have fought against white domination, and I have fought against black domination. I have cherished the ideal of a democratic and free society in which all persons live together in harmony and with equal opportunities. It is an ideal which I hope to live for and to achieve. But if needs be, it is an ideal for which I am prepared to die."

—*April 20, 1964*

THE WONDERS OF OUR WORLD

Caves

Neil Morris

CRABTREE PUBLISHING COMPANY

The Wonders of our World

Crabtree Publishing Company

350 Fifth Avenue, Suite 3308 New York, New York 10118

360 York Road, R. R. 4 Niagara-on-the-Lake, Ontario Canada L0S 1J0

73 Lime Walk Headington, Oxford England 0X3 7AD

Author: Neil Morris
Managing editor: Peter Sackett
Editors: Ting Morris & David Schimpky
Designer: Richard Rowan
Production manager: Graham Darlow
Picture research: Lis Sackett

Picture Credits:
Artists: Martin Camm, Linden Artists
Maps: European Map Graphics Ltd
Photographs: Ardea London 6 (top). Bruce Coleman 3 (bottom left), 14 (bottom), 15 (bottom), 16 (top). CERN 28, 29 (top). Connie Toops 24, (top), 25. A J Eavis 12 (bottom). Frank Lane 3 (bottom right), 5, 10 (top), 11, I5 (bottom), 21, 22. G S F Picture Library 27 (bottom). Jerry Woolridge 9 (bottom), 29 (top). Mary Evans Picture Library 24 (bottom). Robert Harding Picture Library 4, 6 (bottom), 7 (bottom), 8 (bottom), 9, (top), 10 (bottom), 13 (bottom), 19, 23 (bottom). Topham Picturepoint 12 (top), 14 (top), 18 (top).

Cataloging-in-publication data

Morris, Neil
  Caves

(Wonders of our world)
Includes index.
ISBN 0-86505-830-X (library bound) ISBN 0-86505-842-3 (pbk).
This book looks at the natural characteristics of caves, as well as the history and methods of cave exploration.

1. Caves - Juvenile literature. I. Title. II. Series: Morris, Neil. Wonders of our world.

GB601.2.M66 1995   j551.4'47   LC 95-23441

© 1996 Labyrinth Publishing (UK) Ltd.
Created and Produced by Labyrinth Publishing (UK) Ltd in conjunction with Crabtree Publishing Company.

CONTENTS

WHAT IS A CAVE?

A CAVE is a hollow in the ground. This hollow, which we sometimes call a cavern, is really a hole in the earth's crust. Some caves are just below the surface, while others extend deep down into the crust.

Caves can have very long underground passages, with lakes, rivers, and waterfalls. Some caves may be up to 50 million years old. Most developed as water trickled through them, finding paths between layers of rock, filling tunnels, and carving out new passages. Experts have found evidence showing that people and animals have lived in caves since prehistoric times.

BENEATH THE HILLS
An underground world of caves lies beneath the unusual limestone cones and towers of the Shuicheng hills in China.

CAVE ENTRANCE

THE entrance to this big cave in Anshun, China, is huge and easily seen. Sometimes, however, the only evidence of a cave might be a small hole or crack in the ground. Some of the world's most famous caves have been discovered by accident.

INSIDE A CAVE

Constantly dripping water creates fantastic shapes and patterns inside caves, where it is damp, dark, and cold. Amazing sights usually await explorers when they first enter a cave. There are no green plants inside because there is little or no light to help them grow. There are, however, fungi, bacteria, and many other forms of life.

HUGE CAVERNS

SOME CAVES are huge. The main chamber of the famous Carlsbad Caverns in New Mexico is over 1 kilometer (0.6 miles) long and lies over 300 meters (1000 feet) under the ground. This enormous cavern has a ceiling that is as high as a skyscraper in some places. A cowboy discovered the caverns in 1901, when he saw a black cloud rising from a hole in the ground. The cloud was actually a swarm of bats, and the hole was the entrance to a maze of caves.

LIMESTONE AND WATER

THE WORLD'S biggest caves are found in limestone areas. Limestone is a soft rock that dissolves in weak acid. Rainwater contains the acid that eats away at limestone. Over thousands of years, the weak acid nibbles away until thin cracks in the rock grow into bigger holes and then become wide tunnels.

Deep under the ground, the water finally reaches a level called the water table. Here the rock is already full of water and cannot hold any more.

SINKHOLE
Sinkholes are funnel-shaped holes through which water flows into a cave. They usually start as large cracks.

UNDERGROUND RIVER

AS water pours down through the ground, it carves passages from the rock. Water flows through the passages as underground rivers.

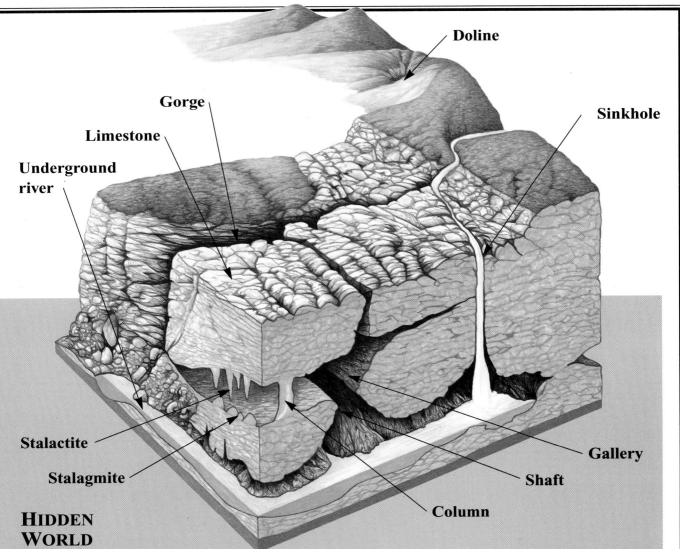

Doline

Sinkhole

Gorge

Limestone

Underground river

Stalactite

Stalagmite

Gallery

Shaft

Column

HIDDEN WORLD

This cross section shows what limestone caves look like under ground. A stream vanishes down a sinkhole, making shafts and galleries. A small doline or large gorge may form when caves collapse.

ACID RAIN

In some areas, acid rain speeds up the formation of caves, as the acidic water widens cracks. Acid rain is a form of pollution caused by gases given off by power plants and factories. Trees and whole forests can be killed by acid rain.

CAVE FORMATIONS

WHEN WATER seeps through limestone, it carries a dissolved mineral called calcite. Over time, this mineral is deposited and creates formations called speleothems.

The best-known speleothems are stalactites, which hang downwards, and stalagmites, which grow upwards. To remember which is which, think "c" is for ceiling in stalactite, and "g" is for ground in stalagmite.

STRANGE SHAPES

A gradual build-up of calcite makes strange shapes. Water drips down from stalactites to make stalagmites. Helictites are spiral shapes, probably caused by wind. Rimstone pools are calcite-rimmed pools of water.

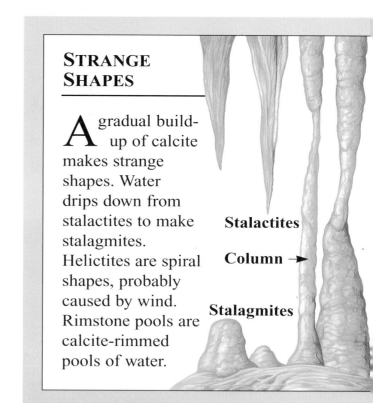

Stalactites

Column →

Stalagmites

CAVE DECORATIONS

Dripping water creates beautiful decorations. As it trickles from cracks in the cave ceiling, the water covers cave walls with flowstone and makes dripstone curtains. The Carlsbad Caverns, in New Mexico, contain huge stalactites and other rock formations.

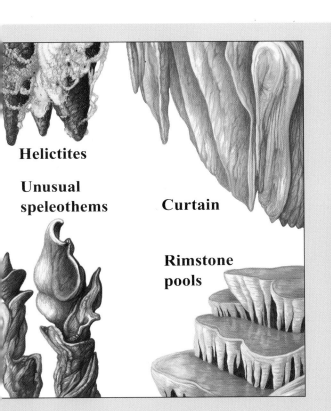

Helictites

Unusual speleothems

Curtain

Rimstone pools

CHRISTMAS TREE

This amazing stalagmite in the Carlsbad Caverns, known as the "Christmas Tree," is 20 meters (65 feet) high.

COLUMNS

STALACTITES and stalagmites can grow together to form a column. These columns are from a cave in China. The world's tallest column, also in China, is 39 meters (128 feet) high! The tallest stalagmite is 32 meters (105 feet) high, and the longest stalactite is over 6 meters (20 feet) in length.

VOLCANIC CAVES

WHEN a volcano erupts, hot molten rock, called lava, is thrown out and flows on the earth's surface. Sometimes, when a river of lava cools and hardens quickly on the outside, the lava inside remains hot and liquid, and flows on. Eventually the lava drains away, leaving a solid, hollow tube.

These volcanic caves, called lava tubes, can easily collapse. Their roof is usually thin, and earthquakes are common in volcanic areas. Lava tubes very rarely last long.

LAVA RIVER
Some volcanoes release streams of lava. These flow as a red-hot river, like this one on Mount Etna, Italy. The surface of the river can cool quickly from contact with cold air and form a hard crust.

KAZIMURA CAVE

THERE are hundreds of volcanic caves in the Hawaiian Islands. Kazimura Cave travels through the earth for more than 11 kilometers (7 miles), making it one of the world's longest lava tubes.

ACTIVE LAVA TUBE

Lava tubes generally have regular shapes with smooth sides. They are usually near the surface, often only about 1 meter (3 feet) under the ground.

These tubes may have many openings in their thin roofs. Stalactites of lava may hang from the ceiling, and the floor may be covered with ripple marks left by the fiery river that created the cave.

ICE CAVES

CAVES CAN form inside glaciers, icebergs, and ice sheets. As a glacier moves slowly toward warmer areas of land, its ice starts to melt. The water which flows under the ice hollows out a cave. These ice caves constantly change their shape and size, and seldom last long.

An ice cave is also formed when meltwater drips into a rock cave and freezes because the cave temperature is very cold. Such caves are filled with amazing ice formations.

DESERT CAVES
There are many deep caves in the mountains of central Asia (left). Although this is desert country, many of these caves are blocked with ice. Some caves in the hot deserts of Arizona and New Mexico are also filled with ice.

ANTARCTIC ICE CAVES

This ice cave is on Ross Island, at the edge of the Ross Ice Shelf, a huge mass of permanent ice in Antarctica. The island is dominated by Mount Erebus, the most southern active volcano in the world. The large cave in this picture has walls of ice, with many long icicles hanging down like stalactites.

ICE GIANTS

E ISRIESEN-WELT, the "world of the ice giants," is a cave system high in the Austrian Alps. It formed over two million years ago when water seeped into the caves and froze into eerie shapes.

Sea Caves

A DIFFERENT type of cave is formed by the sea crashing against rocky cliffs. The pounding action of the waves makes small cracks in the cliffs. The cracks widen as year after year the sea batters them with pebbles and sand. Pieces of rock start to break off and a cave finally forms.

Other sea caves are actually limestone formations under the ocean. The blue holes around the island of Andros, in the Bahamas, lead into a maze of flooded caves. At high tide the shafts fill with water, which makes them look like blue holes in the ocean.

Smugglers' Hideouts
Sea caves were once favorite hideouts for smugglers and pirates because their entrances are often difficult to spot. These caves are in the Outer Hebrides, islands off the northwest coast of Scotland.

BLOWHOLE

WHEN a sea cave fills with water, air inside the cave may be blown out through an opening in the cliff top. As the sea fills a lava cave in Hawaii, air and water shoot out of the Spouting Horn blowhole.

BLUE GROTTO

One of the world's best-known caves is the Blue Grotto, on the Italian island of Capri. Light shining through the cave entrance reflects on the water and becomes blue.

FINGAL'S CAVE

FINGAL'S Cave extends 60 meters (200 feet) into the small Scottish island of Staffa. Its basalt columns formed from cooling lava 60 million years ago.

ANIMALS

INSIDE CAVES it is dark, damp, and usually very cold, yet some creatures spend their whole lives deep inside caves. Because there is little sunlight, many of these animals have white, pale pink or transparent skins. Although some are blind, they can rely on sharp senses of hearing, touch, and smell.

Other animals leave their caves to feed. Many sea caves, for example, are teeming with life. Crayfish, sponges, sea worms, and even sharks live in underwater caverns.

TWINKLING BEETLES
Caves in New Zealand twinkle with thousands of glow-worms. Their bodies radiate light, which attracts the insects on which they feed.

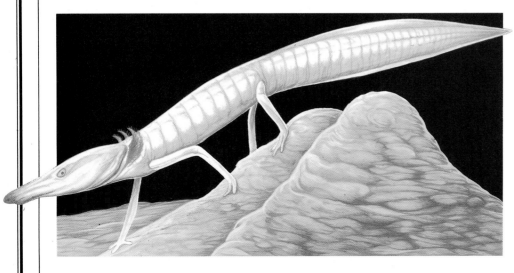

PALE AMPHIBIAN

CAVE-dwelling salamanders can see at birth, but since they never leave their dark cave home their eyelids grow together and their bodies turn pale.

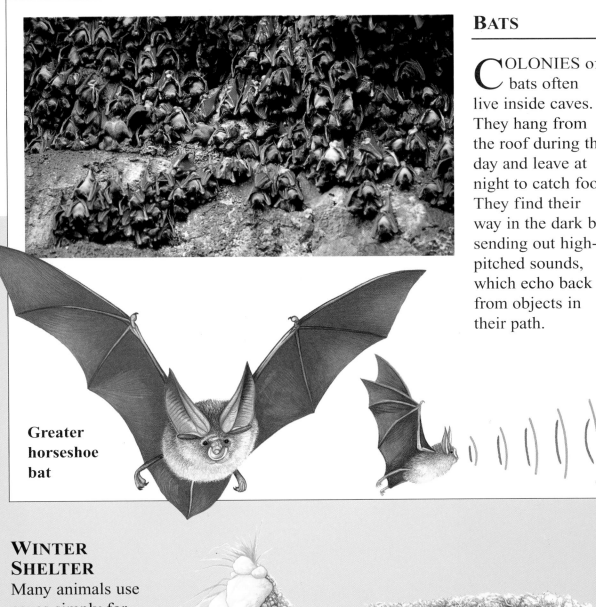

BATS

COLONIES of bats often live inside caves. They hang from the roof during the day and leave at night to catch food. They find their way in the dark by sending out high-pitched sounds, which echo back from objects in their path.

Greater horseshoe bat

WINTER SHELTER

Many animals use caves simply for shelter. When autumn comes, black bears and grizzlies look for a cave in which to sleep through the long winter. Some snakes spend the winter in caves, too.

CAVE PEOPLE

CAVES WERE probably the first homes of people. In China, evidence of cave dwellers takes us back half a million years. Prehistoric humans survived the worst conditions of the last Ice Age by living in caves. Bear skulls found in caves suggest that some early peoples may have worshiped bears and used bear heads in ceremonies.

More recently, caves have been used as shrines. People still inhabit cave houses carved out of volcanic rock in Turkey.

ABORIGINAL PAINTINGS

This cave painting comes from the Arnhem Land region of the Australian Northern Territories. The Aborigine people, the first inhabitants of Australia, passed stories down from generation to generation, often by painting on rock. Some Aborigines continue this tradition.

Arrowhead

Spearhead

Scraper

PREHISTORIC LIFE

PREHISTORIC people used caves not only for shelter, but also for safety from wild animals. Wood was gathered to make fire, which was used for warmth and cooking. Flint from the cave walls provided tools and weapons.

MESA VERDE

These cave dwellings were built in the cliffs at Cortez, in the Mesa Verde region of Colorado. Some of these Native American homes were several stories high. Pueblo people lived here long before Europeans ever came to North America. They dwelt here for over one thousand years, until about AD 1300.

The prehistoric paintings in caves at Lascaux, France, were discovered by four teenage boys in 1940. This is one of over 2000 paintings of bulls, horses, bison, mammoths, and reindeer. They are among the best-preserved prehistoric cave paintings in the world.

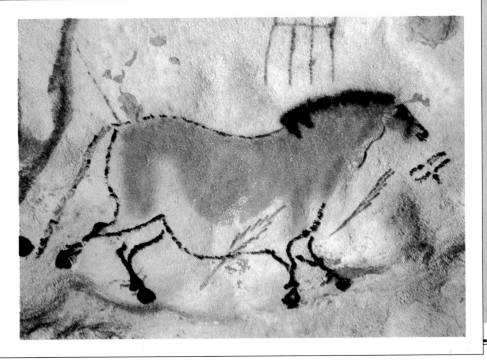

SCIENTIFIC EXPLORATION

THE FIRST account of cave exploration was written by a group of monks in 1002. To make sure they didn't get lost in their underground maze, they unraveled thread as they went. Today, scientists called speleologists use more modern methods to study caves. They have reliable scientific equipment. For major expeditions, underground camps are set up so that scientists can stay down longer.

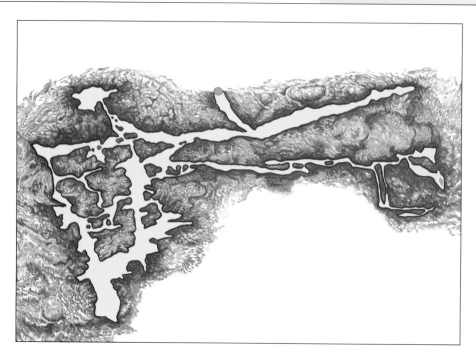

MAPS

AN Austrian professor named Adolf Schmidl made the first accurate cave maps in 1821. Today's maps show the length of tunnels and the height of roofs. This map is a general one of Carlsbad Caverns, New Mexico.

BORNEO EXPEDITION

This cave in Borneo, an island off southeast Asia, is part of a huge network of limestone caves. Cavers exploring there in 1980 discovered a huge cavern that was 700 meters (2300 feet) long and 300 meters (1000 feet) wide. They had found the world's largest cavern.

WORKING UNDER GROUND

Speleologists spend a great deal of time squeezing through small gaps in dark tunnels. They look for minerals and fossils. Fossilized remains of sea creatures are found in many limestone caves. Millions of years ago, present-day inland regions were beneath the ocean.

CAVING

SPELUNKERS are people who enjoy visiting and exploring caves for sport. They always need to be aware that caves can be very dangerous places, especially when rain raises the water level. People should always go into caves in groups, under the guidance of an experienced caver. For dedicated spelunkers, caving is an exciting sport. Only a small number of the world's caves have been explored.

DIVING

SEA-CAVE diving is also popular. Divers wear wetsuits, masks, and flippers. They breathe air using scuba gear. Divers carry lights to penetrate the dark water. They usually take a camera to record what they find.

VERTICAL SHAFTS

Some of the world's deepest caves are over 1500 meters (500 feet) deep. For climbing up and down vertical shafts, called pitches, cavers need strong ropes, metal-runged ladders, winches, and other climbing gear. It is easy to see why caving is a team effort.

Chest harness

Rappel rack

Hand-operated ascender

Caribiner

EQUIPMENT

MOST caving equipment is similar to rock-climbing gear. Cavers wear thick coveralls, helmets, chest harnesses, and climbing boots. They use strong ropes and special clips, but their greatest security lies in good teamwork.

UNDERGROUND HAZARDS

Caving is a tough sport. Spelunkers often struggle through tunnels that are just big enough for their bodies. They crawl through streams and over waterfalls. All the time, there is the danger of the cave roof collapsing! At the end, the cavers are rewarded with seeing caverns filled with the amazing shapes of speleothems.

MAMMOTH CAVE

OVER MILLIONS of years a steady trickle of water has carved a large underground maze from a limestone region in Kentucky. The cave system is called Mammoth Cave because of its enormous size. It is now part of a national park.

Mammoth Cave is the longest system of caves in the world, with a total mapped length of 560 kilometers (347 miles). Some caverns are as big as New York's Grand Central Station! Cave crickets, blindfish, and blind crayfish all live here.

INSIDE THE CAVE
Mummified Native American bodies have been found in the Mammoth Caves. Stone spearheads show that Native people used these caves nearly 4000 years ago.

TOURISM

ONE OF the two natural entrances to the caves was found in 1797 by a hunter chased by a bear. The caves' first explorer and guide was Stephen Bishop, a slave. By the 1850s, the caves had become a popular tourist attraction.

FANTASTIC FORMATIONS

THE GIGANTIC caverns are full of natural stone formations. "Frozen Niagara" has colorful stalagmites and stalactites that look like a waterfall turned to stone. Other attractions are the "Pillars of Hercules," "Giant's Coffin," and a narrow passage known as "Fat Man's Misery." These formations are now illuminated by spotlights for tourists.

DEEPEST CAVES

THERE ARE many deep caves all over the world that have yet to be explored. The map on the opposite page shows where the world's deepest caves are located.

Modern caving equipment allows cavers to explore deeper than ever before. Scientific tests, however, have shown that some of the world's deepest caves extend further into the earth than humans have explored. It is thought that a cave in Italy may be over 1800 meters (5900 feet) deep.

SMALL ENTRANCE
This entrance leads to the Bol-Bulok cave in central Asia. The cave's main passage is over 1,300 meters (4265 feet) long, but it is no more than half a meter (20 inches) wide.

WINDY CAVE
Cavers call the main river passage of Pierre-Saint-Martin cave, in the Pyrenees mountains of France, "windy tunnel." Certain weather conditions on the surface cause a strong wind to blow through this very deep cave.

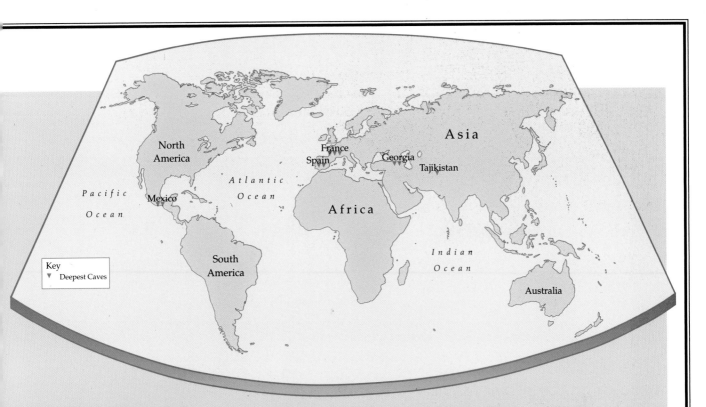

WHERE THEY ARE

1. **Réseau Jean Bernard, France: 1602 m (5256 ft.)**
2. **Shakta Pantjukhina, Georgia: 1508 m (4947 ft.)**
3. **Sistema Huautla, Mexico: 1476 m (4842 ft.)**
4. **Sistema del Trave, Spain: 1441· m (4728 ft.)**
5. **Aminakoateak, Spain: 1408 m (4619 ft.)**
6. **Snezhnaya, Georgia: 1370 m (4495 ft.)**
7. **Réseau Pierre-Saint-Martin, France: 1342 m (4403 ft.)**
8. **Bol-Bulok, Tajikistan: 1315 m (4314 ft.)**
9. **Sistema Cuicateca, Mexico: 1243 m (4078 ft.)**
10. **Gouffre Berger, France: 1242 m (4075 ft.)**

GOUFFRE BERGER

THESE CAVES, in France, are among the world's deepest. Cavers exploring the caverns find fascinating formations, such as these giant, smooth steps in the rock.

TODAY AND TOMORROW

THE WORLD'S caves are constantly changing due to the effects of water, so research and exploration will always continue. There will be new, deeper, and longer caves to visit and study.

Scientists find caves and human-made tunnels useful in their work. Caves have helped us catch rare particles from the sun, and perhaps they will contribute towards new discoveries in the future.

SCIENCE UNDERGROUND

A GREAT deal of scientific research can be done inside natural caves. Scientists set up laboratories to find out how underground conditions affect their experiments. This huge piece of apparatus in a Swiss cave (right) measures heat accurately.

Surveys of rocks, minerals, and fossils found beneath the Earth's surface help scientists understand the make-up of our planet and how it might have been formed billions of years ago. Geologists also explore the Earth for coal, oil, gas, uranium, and other sources of energy.

ATOMIC RESEARCH

IN Switzerland scientists use equipment in a human-made underground tunnel (left) to crash atomic particles into each other at high speeds. The circles (right) show the location of the research tunnels.

POWER STATION

This is part of Dinorwig power station. It was built in a tunnel deep inside a mountain in Snowdonia, north Wales, in the United Kingdom. Water released from storage tanks rushes through turbines. The force of the water turning the turbines is used to make electricity.

GLOSSARY

Acid A chemical substance that eats away at solid materials.

Bacteria Tiny single-cell organisms.

Basalt The most common volcanic rock.

Blowhole A hole in the roof of a sea cave where air and water shoot out.

Calcite A mineral deposited in limestone caves by water; composed of calcium carbonate.

Crust The hard outer layer of the earth.

Doline A funnel-shaped hollow in the ground.

Dripstone A kind of calcite rock formation found on cave walls.

Flowstone A kind of calcite rock formation found on cave walls.

Fossil The preserved remains of prehistoric animals and plants.

Fungi Plural of fungus; very simple living things, such as mushrooms.

Gallery A room-like underground passage.

Geologist A scientist who studies the natural history and structure of the earth.

Glacier A slowly moving mass of ice.

Gorge A deep ravine.

Helictite A spiral-shaped rock formation found in caves.

Ice Age A time, long ago, when much of the earth was covered by ice.

Iceberg A large mass of ice floating in the sea.

Lava Molten rock that pours out of a volcano.

Limestone	A soft rock that dissolves in weak acid.
Meltwater	Melted snow or ice.
Mineral	A solid substance that occurs naturally in the earth.
Mummy	A body specially prepared for burial so that it will be preserved.
Neutrino	A rare particle from the sun or another star.
Pitch	A vertical shaft, or drop, in a cave.
Prehistoric	Relating to ancient times before writing was invented.
Rimstone	A calcite rock formation around a pool of water in a cave.
Scuba gear	Breathing apparatus with air cylinders used by divers.
Shaft	A vertical underground passage.
Shrine	A place of worship.
Sinkhole	A funnel-shaped hole in the ground, where water flows into a cave.
Speleologist	A scientist who studies caves.
Speleothem	A cave rock formation, such as a stalactite, caused by dripping water which carries and deposits calcite.
Spelunker	A person who explores caves as a sport or hobby.
Stalactite	A rock formation hanging from the ceiling of a cave.
Stalagmite	A rock formation sticking up from the floor of a cave.
Volcano	An opening where molten rock and gas come from inside the earth.
Water table	The underground level where rocks are full of water.

INDEX

123456789 Printed in the U.S.A. 432109876